AF602039

Palgrave Socio-Legal Studies

Series Editor
Dave Cowan
School of Law
University of Bristol
Bristol, UK

More information about this series at
http://www.palgrave.com/gp/series/14679

Didi Herman • Connal Parsley
Editors

Interdisciplinarities

Research Process, Method, and the Body of Law

Editors
Didi Herman
Kent Law School
University of Kent
Canterbury, UK

Connal Parsley
Kent Law School
University of Kent
Canterbury, UK

Palgrave Socio-Legal Studies
ISBN 978-3-030-89296-8 ISBN 978-3-030-89297-5 (eBook)
https://doi.org/10.1007/978-3-030-89297-5

Cover illustration: Kevin White / Alamy Stock Photo

This Palgrave Macmillan imprint is published by the registered company Springer Nature Switzerland AG.
The registered company address is: Gewerbestrasse 11, 6330 Cham, Switzerland

Acknowledgements

We first thank our contributors for their willingness to take on an unusual task and to stick with it (and us) despite a global pandemic, and to respond so helpfully to our feedback. We are very grateful to them. Thanks are due also to Dave Cowan, in whose series this volume appears, for his interest in and enthusiasm for this project. Marie Selwood provided us with expert editorial assistance and was a delight to work with. We would also like to thank Josie Taylor at Palgrave and Rubina Infanta Rani at Springer for all their help and understanding throughout the process. Last but not least, we thank Kent Law School for its support from the early stages to the final ones.

Praise for *Interdisciplinarities*

"Research is never the 'plug and play' that conventional methods books describe. Affirming the messiness and contingency of real projects, this book places us in the joyful, vexing, fleshy life of the 'how' of research, offering lessons for new and veteran scholars alike."

—Nicholas Blomley FRCS, *Professor of Geography, Simon Fraser University, Canada*

"This innovative and groundbreaking volume focuses on the messiness of *how* to do research and the various ways scholars approach their subject-matter, often making personal and idiosyncratic decisions in the process of *doing*. The reflective and exploratory mode of inquiry is vitally important, reminding us all of the embedded biases within what we like to think of as objective legal scholarship."

—Eve Darian-Smith, *Professor and Chair, Global and International Studies, University of California, Irvine, USA*

"*Interdisciplinarities* offers an entirely fresh perspective on socio-legal research methods. Stemming from a challenge given to a group of scholars, the authors at one level illustrate a wide variety of situated approaches to interdisciplinary research methods. More importantly, however, the work brings the researching body as subject and object into the very heart of the question of method. At times intensely personal, often inspirational, and always highly reflective and readable, the chapters collectively demystify and locate method in a way which will encourage us all to reflect on our own research experiences and practices."

—Margaret Davies, *Matthew Flinders Distinguished Professor, College of Business, Government and Law, Flinders University, Australia*

"There is not enough attention to "process" in publishing. We academics are all about the product: finished, polished, done. But interdisciplinarity is itself a process and in this fantastic volume authors write about their own processes, embodied and worldly, during a world-wide pandemic, while reflecting on the place of the body in law and legal studies. This brilliant volume should be read by those interested in law's interdisciplinarities but also by anyone who writes and has a body."

—Bonnie Honig, *Nancy Duke Lewis Professor, Political Science and Modern Culture and Media (MCM), Brown University, USA*

Contents

1 **Introduction** 1
Connal Parsley and Didi Herman

2 **Archived Bodies: The Transatlantic Slave Trade and Abolition** 9
Emily Haslam

3 **Bodies, Medicine and Otherness** 23
Emilie Cloatre

4 **Researching Racialised Bodies in Higher Education: From Statistics to Storytelling** 37
Suhraiya Jivraj

5 **Exploring the Law/Bodies/Space Regulatory Conundrum** 53
Helen Carr

6 **Reading the Body That Was Not Written** 73
Thanos Zartaloudis

7 **Working with an Example of the Body: Legal Thinking as Method in Interdisciplinary Cultural Studies** 87
Connal Parsley

8 **~~Cross-Disciplinarity as a Practice of Critical Linking: How Does a Scholar Relate Different 'Bodies'~~? Writing from Within the Body as a Research Process** 107
Hyo Yoon Kang

9 **Afterword** 127
Davina Cooper

Notes on Contributors

Helen Carr is Professor in Law at University of Southampton Law School. She has authored many articles in the areas of housing, homelessness and social care, which have appeared in many publications. Her work is socio-legal, theoretically informed and motivated by a concern for social justice. Her most recent book is *Law and the Precarious Home* (Bloomsbury, 2020, edited with Brendan Edgeworth and Caroline Hunter). She also sits as a fee paid judge with the First Tier Tribunal (Property) Chamber.

Emilie Cloatre is Professor in Law at Kent Law School. She is a socio-legal scholar whose main research interests lie in the intersection between law and contemporary 'science and society' issues, including pharmaceutical flows, access to health, and the regulation of alternative and traditional medicine. Her approach to law is influenced by insights from Science and Technology Studies and, in particular, by actor–network theory. Her publications include *Pills for the Poorest: An Exploration of TRIPS and Access to Medicines in Sub-Saharan Africa* (Palgrave Macmillan, 2013) and *Knowledge, Technology and Law* (2014, edited with Martyn Pickersgill). She is Principal Investigator for a five-year Wellcome Trust project (2017–2022) entitled 'Law, Knowledges and the Making of "Modern" Healthcare: Regulating Traditional and Alternative Medicines in Contemporary Contexts'.

Davina Cooper is Research Professor in Law and Political Theory at Dickson Poon School of Law, King's College London. Her interdisciplinary work focuses on radical forms of state and non-state governance and on prefigurative conceptualising. She is the author of six books, including *Feeling Like a State* (Duke University Press, 2019) and *Everyday Utopias* (Duke University Press, 2014). From 2018 to 2022, she led an ESRC-funded research project on 'The Future of Legal Gender'; and from 2004 to 2009, she directed the AHRC Research Centre in Law, Gender & Sexuality.

Emily Haslam is Senior Lecturer in International Law and a co-director of the Centre for Critical International Law at Kent Law School where she teaches international law, and international and transnational criminal law. Her research interests lie in the fields of international criminal law, international legal history, civil society, and slavery and abolition. She is the author of *The Slave Trade, Abolition and the Long History of Criminal Law* (Routledge, 2019).

Didi Herman is Emeritus Professor at the University of Kent. Her work has appeared in many publications in the fields of social movements and law reform, gender and sexuality, race and racism, and Israel/Palestine.

Suhraiya Jivraj is Reader in Law and Social Justice at Kent Law School and Senior Fellow of the Higher Education Academy (SFHEA). Her previous experience includes working for international NGOs and grassroots organisations in the human rights and anti-discrimination fields. She teaches and researches in the areas of public law including human rights, race, religion and law, intersectional and decolonial approaches to equalities law and policy, and social justice. Her work draws on critical race/religion theories and de-colonial studies, exploring contemporary socio-legal problematics including intersecting inequalities, foregrounding feminist/queer of colour perspectives. She is the author of *The Religion of Law* (Palgrave Macmillan, 2013).

Hyo Yoon Kang is Reader in Law at Kent Law School. She has conducted extensive and far-reaching research at the intersection of intellectual property, history of sciences, political economy, law and humanities, and legal and critical theory. See www.hyoyoonkang.com for more information.

Connal Parsley is Senior Lecturer in Law at Kent Law School. His research spans the fields of critical jurisprudence, political theory and visual cultural studies. The author of numerous articles on the work of Giorgio Agamben, he has also translated several texts from Italian, including Roberto Esposito *Categories of the Impolitical* (Fordham University Press 2015). He is the co-director of the AHRC network on Law and the Human, which investigates the figure of the human in law in light of contemporary scientific, political, environmental and technological change.

Thanos Zartaloudis is Reader in Legal Theory and History at Kent Law School; doctoral advisor at the Architectural Association, School of Architecture, London; and a visiting professor at Harvard University, Center for Hellenic Studies. His most recent book is *The Birth of Nomos* (Edinburgh University Press 2019), and he is the editor of the recent collection titled *Law and Philosophical Theory: Critical Intersections* (Rowman & Littlefield 2019). He is also the head editor (with Anton Schütz) of the book series titled *Encounters in Law and Philosophy* (Edinburgh University Press).

CHAPTER 1

Introduction

Connal Parsley and Didi Herman

Abstract This chapter introduces the project of this edited collection, which takes a new approach to interdisciplinary legal research methods. The book investigates how scholars go about their work, while situating their practical choices within a wider context of conceptual and methodological meaning-making. Contributors were asked: if you were tasked with writing a hypothetical chapter on 'the body', where would you start? What would be your next steps, and why? Which literatures would you draw upon, and how would the process unfold given your choices? The chapter introduces the contributions, drawing out commonalities and differences in their chosen starting points; the 'mess', limitations and situatedness of research processes themselves; and their 'end points'—goals, motivations, and what they hope to achieve. It concludes that interdisciplinary research involves choices around discipline and method that are deeply personal, and speak to the connectedness and inherently ethical nature of research practice.

Keywords Legal studies • Interdisciplinary research • Research method • Research process • Research messiness

C. Parsley (✉) • D. Herman
Kent Law School, University of Kent, Canterbury, UK
e-mail: c.parsley@kent.ac.uk; d.herman@kent.ac.uk

D. Herman, C. Parsley (eds.), *Interdisciplinarities*, Palgrave Socio-Legal Studies, https://doi.org/10.1007/978-3-030-89297-5_1

Background

This collection of chapters emerged out of a workshop held at Kent Law School (KLS) in November 2018. We planned the workshop to showcase the diverse range of interdisciplinary scholars active in KLS, with a particular focus on methods—the *how* of research, more than the *what*. Our intention was for participants to strip away the layers of 'final product' that often hide the choices and assumptions about discipline and methods that underlie it and, in a sense, to reveal the initial scaffolding they put in place.

We wanted contributors to 'show not tell', and so the workshop was not intended to explore the meanings (or existence) of 'interdisciplinarity'; nor were participants asked to explain their particular research methods in generic terms. To further this end, we gave them a very specific mandate for the workshop:

If asked to write a paper for an edited collection entitled *Bodies*:

1. What is your first thought?
2. Where would you decide to start and why (i.e. how would you formulate the questions you want to ask, and why these questions)?
3. What's your next step and why?
4. What are your 'go to' literatures, and what do you think the limitations of these writings might be?
5. How do you think the rest of this task will unfold, and can you reflect on how, if you'd made other choices, it might unfold differently?

The workshop went well, and we decided to bring it to the 2019 Socio-Legal Studies Association conference. Following that session, Dave Cowan invited us to submit a book proposal to his series with Palgrave Macmillan. The contract for this collection was finalised in autumn of 2019 for publication in 2021. As with so much academic work during the pandemic, the book was delayed for nearly a year. Indeed, SARS-CoV-2 now forms an important backdrop to several of the chapters.

Approaching Method

Much work about interdisciplinary legal methods tends to approach its subject descriptively—this is 'law and economics'; this is 'feminist legal method', and so on. As a result, these texts tend to list a range of possible methods, posing interdisciplinarity as the combination of one or more self-contained disciplines, each with its relatively clear 'rules'. Recent texts include Dawn Watkins and Mandy Burton's *Research Methods in Law* (2017), Mike McConville and Wing Hong Chui's *Research Methods for Law* (2017) (both now in their second editions), P. Ishwara Bhat's 627-page *Ideas and Methods in Legal Research* (2019), and Emilios Christodoulidis et al.'s *Research Handbook on Critical Legal Theory* (2019). These volumes function as resource handbooks, largely providing readers with examples of different ways of doing legal research. At times, it can be tempting to understand such research methods as pre-existing paths that can or should be followed as a way to ensure research quality or efficacy. At other times, the methodological questions can be presented as 'legal theoretical' problems—for example, as ways of understanding legal thinking and activity, or as a heuristic for mapping relations between law, the humanities, and the social or hard sciences. Andreas Philippopoulos-Mihalopoulos's collection *Routledge Handbook of Law and Theory* (2018) is more in this latter category, as are some of the contributions to the early part of Naomi Creutzfeldt et al.'s *Routledge Handbook of Socio-legal Theory and Methods* (2020).

This book is different, perhaps more in the tradition of John Law's *After Method* (2004), or Simon Halliday and Patrick Schmidt's *Conducting Law and Society Research* (2009), both of which are rooted in the 'messiness' of research. The authors in this volume draw on their practical, personal research experiences to address a hypothetical research task, while also placing those experiences in the wider context of conceptual and methodological meaning-making. The common thematic device uniting the contributions, 'the body', has been a central theme in successive waves of legal scholarship, as well as in the diverse related fields on which that scholarship has drawn. Still today, as seen by the breadth of references in the contributions to this volume, it is interrogated, positioned and leveraged in innumerable ways, under the influence of political and ethical commitments, disciplinary concerns, and changing technological and ecological conditions of contemporary life.[1]

This centrality and multiplicity of 'the body' allows the collection to trace a number of rich approaches into the *process* of research as practised by these diverse scholars. It presents a terrain on which choices must be made by authors and offers a (relatively) stable point of reference through which those choices become more visible and comparable, despite also highlighting their idiosyncratic nature. The book thus offers a self-reflective, somewhat 'meta' view on the body, as well as taking a fresh approach to the historically vexed problem of research methodology in legal studies. While each contributor exemplifies this process-based approach in their own way, the collection as a whole allows readers to discern the different kinds of choices scholars make as they map out divergent trajectories of what begins as the same path.

KLS is home to a wide variety of legal research. Its scholars analyse a broad spectrum of legal issues and contexts, taking diverse approaches to law from across the humanities and social sciences. Some of these are represented in this volume, but the aim here is not to cover particular fields or methods, nor the range of work being undertaken at KLS. It might have been possible to arrange the volume by categorising the contributions as 'socio-legal approaches', 'law and history', 'critical race studies', and so on. Instead, we hope that the contributions to this book demonstrate how choices about methods and frameworks are emergent, idiosyncratic and context-dependent. While all the authors have

[1] For just one such example, see Chris Dietz et al. (2020) *A Jurisprudence of the Body*.

(multi)disciplinary 'comfort zones', 'methodology', for them, is not about a kind of 'law and …' rule-following, but is about being curious, adaptable, and acknowledging the messiness, instability and unpredictability of research and writing. In this sense, these essays demonstrate that the *how* of research is also an inherently ethical process, as we discuss further below.

The Contributions

Starting Points

Although occasionally self-evident, where we begin with a piece of research is often opaque within the finished product. For some of our contributors, a pre-existing research project provided the impetus for how they would go about writing a chapter on 'the body'. Emilie Cloatre, Emily Haslam, and Suhraiya Jivraj all begin their task by rooting themselves in a foundation of materials and concepts they had already developed: long-standing projects on alternative healing, the slave trade and decolonising higher education respectively. They all tell the reader a little about these projects and then explore the particular concerns and challenges posed by 'the body chapter' task. Helen Carr, on the other hand, begins by reflecting on her dual roles as an academic and a housing tribunal member, and with a memory triggered by the task itself. Her next step would be to undertake a 'scoping' of the terrain.

Hyo Yoon Kang tells the reader immediately that she was unable to write the intended chapter due to a serious injury, and that she will instead write *from within* the body rather than *about* it: 'The reason for the unusual format is that my body became the subject rather than the object of academic thinking about methodology.' Thanos Zartaloudis also begins with some personal biography, but, like Kang, his major interest would be in exploring 'the body' conceptually, in his case as part of an explicit rejection of the dualism of subject versus nature or matter. Connal Parsley reflects on his past writing and teaching, considering whether there is anything there to adapt or extend. He concludes that the hypothetical chapter could make a methodological contribution to an ongoing project on 'law, technology and the notion of the "human" '.

Whether authors start with a problematic, a question, a memory, or a concept, most use the task, at least in part, to reflect explicitly on their own 'positionality' as researchers. They explore whether the task falls outside their 'comfort zone' (Cloatre, Haslam), how the hypothetical book's unifying theme speaks to their own bodily experiences (Jivraj, Kang, Zartaloudis), how Covid impacted on their work (Cloatre, Kang), or how the research process is often 'messy' and difficult to discipline (Carr, Cloatre, Parsley, Zartaloudis). For those chapters rooted in pre-existing projects, the research materials authors intend to rely on include interviews and case studies (Carr, Cloatre), fiction (Carr), a singular example (Parsley), first person accounts (Jivraj) and historical texts, including their limitations and silences (Haslam, Zartaloudis). These materials shape the exploratory methods the authors choose. Kang's primary material is her new fiction and non-fiction reading on pain.

All the contributors (with one exception) make clear that their thinking would be initially propelled by scholarly literatures beyond 'law properly so-called' with which they are already familiar. These include governmentality (Carr); science and technology studies (Cloatre); critical histories of slavery and archives (Haslam); critical race theory (Jivraj); Agamben, cultural anthropology and art history (Parsley); and the Western philosophical canon (Zartaloudis). Kang's chapter stands apart here as she expresses a frustration with some forms of theorising in the first year of the Covid pandemic and, instead, draws her inspiration from new reading on pain and grief.

Along the Journey

Authors were asked to make visible their 'research choices' as they go along, and, in order to proceed with this task, several want to know: who is the intended reader of the edited collection? Which of several possible examples will best suit the book's themes? How prescriptive will the editors be? Might some of the authors I discuss read this piece? Should I tell the editors I'm struggling and may need to pull out? Some also express concerns about the constraints of the book chapter format, and their own limitations in terms of time and knowledge base.

Several contributors observe how 'messy' and unpredictable their research process is: 'In my career to date, the papers that took longest to come together are not the ones that I had initially thought would prove most difficult, and vice versa' (Cloatre). Carr writes: 'I need to remind myself to focus.' Both Parsley and Zartaloudis describe similar journeys of scribbled note-taking, materials-hoarding, prolonged reading, culminating in a sudden burst of writing: 'One is not in control' (Zartaloudis). Kang, in her chapter, relates an experience of disintegration:

> Dream feels most natural, as if I am more awake than in an awake state, a sentence pre-utterance or voicing is German, Korean, English, all mixed. Even single words come out mixed now. There is no 'official' me in 'me' able to be expressed by language at this point; only a very soft body.

Another striking theme to which several contributors keep returning is a concern with research ethics and 'doing justice'.[2] For Cloatre, this imperative relates most directly to her research subjects, particularly alternative healer informants—especially when they are engaged in activities of questionable value or ones deemed illegal by the state. Jivraj explains that the choice of research methods for this hypothetical 'body' chapter would be rooted in her

[2] Doing justice is also a concern for the editors, our hope being to do justice to these contributions in this 'Introduction'.

ethical commitment to prioritise the voices of those often left out of mainstream discourse on 'racial attainment gaps' in higher education. Haslam discusses the ethical responsibility she may have to the long-dead persons described in official archives, and how understandings of these duties can change during the research and writing process. Parsley hopes to do justice to 'the example': the thing he engages with to make his arguments (i.e. a document or an artwork). An example 'is something that asserts itself and asks to be taken more seriously'. Echoing Kang, he writes that it 'asks to be "thought with", rather than thought about', while respecting the various kinds of agency at play within its subject matter and cultural forms. Kang's chapter can be read in its entirety as a meditation on the impossibility of 'doing justice' to the body in pain. Concerns with pain and suffering, and a researcher's ethical responsibilities to 'represent' it (or not), also appear in several other contributions (Haslam, Jivraj, Parsley, Zartaloudis).

The End Point

Why do we write what we write? In the case of a hypothetical book within a book, answering that question has two parts. First, our contributors may have agreed to attempt the task because we asked them. In other words, collegiality and generosity were their primary motivations. This impetus is perhaps even clearer when, as some authors note, chapters such as these may not be obvious entries for the UK's Research Excellence Framework assessment scheme. More and more, with a background of national research assessment and increasingly demanding promotion processes, academics choose carefully what sorts of writing they do and for which outlets. Contemplation, ethical responsibilities and self-doubt underlie all of our writing processes but are rarely articulated as they are in this collection. But our contributors also consider the 'why' of the hypothetical chapter. What is it that motivates them to do this particular piece of work? That all are driven, in part, by intellectual curiosity is obvious. But what would they aim to achieve with their chapter? Each author expresses their end goal in different ways, some more explicitly than others.

Carr identifies three potential aims to her hypothetical contribution: discovering relationships between concepts, things and everyday experience; developing an interpretive lens to understand 'home making/unmaking/remaking'; and constructing a genealogy or architecture of 'how the law constitutes and is constituted by particular understandings of the body': 'whose bodies are protected and why'. She also wants her work to be 'useful' to other academics, to precarious housing tenants, and to housing regulators and professionals. Haslam also discusses the different possible end points opened up by the hypothetical task. For her, these include bringing a legal lens to a non-legal literature and/or the reverse; using archival materials to expose contemporary slavery practices; and contributing to existing debates about reparations or the limits of legal emancipation. Fundamentally, however, Haslam hopes to do 'narrative justice' by providing 'an account which would emphasise the resistance and agency of enslaved and liberated Africans'—that would be her primary aim.

Jivraj, in keeping with her broader project on decolonisation, would want to 'expose power in knowledge production' and contribute to 'meaningful change'. Her methodological choices would be anchored in end point commitments to 'empower bodies of colour', 'explore the impact of racialisation on bodies of colour', and 'make space' for racialised bodies to 'speak' in a context where they are normally reduced to percentage gaps. For Cloatre, the chapter, as part of her larger project on alternative healing, would hope to illustrate 'how the work done by legal and biomedical institutions comes to construct particular lines of tolerance'. Like Carr, her aim would be to understand how and why institutions regulate some bodies and not others. Unlike the other contributors, she notes that her chapter would definitely be a co-authored one, as the project as a whole is being co-produced by several researchers, and so 'authorial aims' would not just be her own.

Zartaloudis tells us what he is *not* interested in achieving: 'I do not pre-emptively serve a particular set of politics or other viewpoints'—an idea that combines with his definition of 'theory' as 'the way in which we as a species are open to the world, irreparably and without totality or end'. In contrast to some of the other contributors, Zartaloudis arrives at his primary research question at the very end of his chapter—his final place becomes his starting place; fittingly so perhaps, given the hypothetical chapter's focus on resurrection.

Parsley also explicitly notes that some of the most salient insights may occur at the very end of his process. Throughout the chapter, he articulates a variety of aims, including 'to discuss in detail how a particular representation of the body "works" ', while reflexively addressing how techniques of legal thinking can be repurposed for interdisciplinary cultural studies, enabling counter-readings. While he hopes this might be useful to others working with humanities approaches to law, what is perhaps most striking is how self-testing his research process is. He speaks repeatedly of challenging himself; finding his own limits, and those of his 'example'.

Kang's contribution would suggest that she cannot formulate aims for her hypothetical chapter in the context of enduring severe physical pain, being a body, literally, unable to write. However, the idea of 'the body' sparks an intellectual and visceral wandering, drawing on a wide range of sources. Her essay culminates in a proposal that the hypothetical chapter would offer 'an initial diagnosis of the dialectical aspects of the ways in which we use the word "body"', and she concludes with a memory of birth.

Through accepting our invitation, our contributors have, to varying degrees, exposed an internal dialogue that all researchers engage in during a particular writing project. More conventional approaches to 'interdisciplinary methodologies' tend to offer a disciplined product, where the more private, existential questions about how and why we make the choices we do are submerged. This collection offers a different understanding of the research process, one that explicitly acknowledges its messiness, its limitations and inadequacies, its unpredictability and its vulnerabilities. For us as scholars, the research process, including its choices around 'disciplines' and 'methods', is deeply personal, and humming with anxiety. But the contributions to this collection also show us that it can equally be an experience of surprise, experimentation, intellectual excitement, pleasure, joy, challenge and meaning-making—that these, too, are the 'why' of why we do what we do, well beyond the stated 'aims and objectives' of published work. Fundamentally, these contributions are about intense forms of connectedness—to ourselves and others, to our 'objects', to our own and other disciplines, and to doing justice to all of these bodies.

References

Bhat, P. I. (2019). *Idea and Methods of Legal Research*. Oxford University Press.

Christodoulidis, E., Dukes, R., & Goldoni, M. (2019). *Research Handbook on Critical Legal Theory*. Edward Elgar.

Creutzfeldt, N., Mason, M., & McConnachie, K. (Eds.). (2020). *Routledge Handbook of Socio-legal Theory and Methods*. Routledge.

Dietz, C., Mitchell, T., & Thomson, M. (Eds.). (2020). *A Jurisprudence of the Body*. Palgrave Macmillan.

Halliday, S., & Schmidt, P. (2009). *Conducting Law and Society Research: Reflections on Methods and Practices*. Cambridge University Press.

Law, J. (2004). *After Method: Mess in Social Science Research*. Routledge.

McConville, M., & Chui, W. H. (Eds.). (2017). *Research Methods for Law* (2nd ed.). Edinburgh University Press.

Philippopoulos-Mihalopoulos, A. (Ed.). (2018). *Routledge Handbook of Law and Theory*. Routledge.

Watkins, D., & Burton, M. (Eds.). (2017). *Research Methods in Law* (2nd ed.). Routledge.

CHAPTER 2

Archived Bodies: The Transatlantic Slave Trade and Abolition

Emily Haslam

Abstract In this contribution, I reflect on law and the body in the context of the transatlantic slave trade and abolition, focusing on law's role in the commodification of the body, on the one hand, and the resistance of slaves and liberated Africans to and/or through law on the other. I draw on critical approaches to the archive, a body of literature which sheds vital light on silences in history, and provides inspiration for thinking about what is at stake in responding to silences. The contribution articulates some of the political, personal and ethical choices that underpin research and writing on a legal history of the body in this context and some of the contemporary implications of the narratives that might result.

Keywords Slavery • Abolition • Legal history • Commodification and resistance • Archival research • Humanities methodologies

My thanks go to the editors, Didi Herman and Connal Parsley, and to Suhraiya Jivraj for their comments on earlier drafts.

E. Haslam (✉)
University of Kent, Canterbury, UK
e-mail: e.haslam@kent.ac.uk

D. Herman, C. Parsley (eds.), *Interdisciplinarities*, Palgrave Socio-Legal Studies, https://doi.org/10.1007/978-3-030-89297-5_2

Introduction

My starting point for a potential contribution to an edited collection on the body would be to reflect on the role of law in the commodification of the body in the context of the transatlantic slave trade. I would also be interested in the ways people resisted the body's commodification and the role that law played variously as an object, or alternatively a tool, of resistance to such commodification. My focus would be on the resistance of enslaved and liberated Africans. Over the past few years, I have worked with archival material at the National Archives, Kew (Haslam, 2019). Working with archives has been variously exciting, engrossing, exhausting and frustrating. My starting point would be to return to these—and different—sources—with a different central focus, that of the body.

When I first embarked on exploring sources at the National Archives, I was naively lured by the thought of uncovering 'hidden' narratives. Moreover, handling 200-year-old documents provided a more physical research experience than what has otherwise—for me at least—become largely a search through electronic databases, rewarding in its own way of course. Through dusty boxes, faded ink, rough paper, margin notes and multiple drafts of documents, this tangible experience gave the impression of making more real my connection with the 'past' and its documentary determinacy, indeterminacy and contingency. Very quickly, and with deeper engagement with critical literature on the archive, I realised that the archive was not simply a site where hitherto 'hidden' voices could speak and be heard. It is in reconciling the tension between the limits of the sources and this desire for discovery or an alternative way of narration that I find critical approaches to the archive vitally illuminating.

My approach to legal history and historical methodology in general then has been heavily influenced by critical approaches to the archive and history writing. A number of scholars (Scott, 2004; Stoler, 2009; Mawani, 2012; Trouillot, 2015) have significantly influenced my thinking. Such scholars call on us to interrogate the power relations behind the construction of particular bodies of knowledge as authoritative as well as those that lie behind the creation of the archive and its sources in the first place (Trouillot, 2015). As Renisa Mawani explains, the archive is not just 'a repository of historical records and sources but a dynamic, incomplete and fiercely disputed site of knowledge production that carries profound implications for how we write history and approach and understand the past' (Mawani, 2012, p 339). These approaches are particularly appropriate for exploring how law and the colonial legal archive silence enslaved and liberated Africans as well as for providing tools for thinking about alternative possible accounts about individuals and, more specifically here, their relationships to law. For all these reasons, critical approaches to the archive are my 'go to' literature on the nature of archival research and history writing more generally. However, although my focus is historical, these techniques are not restricted to the past. Critical approaches to the archive can provide techniques for reading and thinking about contemporary cases, legal sources and research more generally.

As an international lawyer trained in English law, I would be thinking about the slave trade and the body in the context of international and/or English Law. Britain was a major slave-trading state. Although at the beginning of the nineteenth century Britain was the main state pushing for slave trade abolition on the international level,[1] British slave traders had first trafficked at least 2.6 million Africans to the Americas (Hamilton & Shaikh, 2012, p 2). Although there is evidence that British involvement in the slave trade continued after abolition (Sherwood, 2007), Britain exerted disproportionate impact on the development of the international law of slave trade abolition, in part enabled through its naval hegemony. There is therefore a natural synergy in examining the body and the law in the context of the transatlantic slave trade and its abolition in English and international law. But that still leaves open the question of the particular focus of my contribution, an issue that raises practical and more politically infused questions about the nature of legal history writing—and its ability to speak to the present—which this contribution explores.

There are many different ways an account about law and its relations with the body in the context of the slave trade might be narrated. First, I would need to decide to what ends am I making my contribution. In the first instance, this will be determined by the particular aims of the volume. Whilst contributing to an edited collection to some extent channels my research focus to someone else's agenda, it also provides a potentially productive opportunity for me to approach my existing research from an alternative perspective. I will need to reflect how any contribution I might make 'fits' with those of other contributors. For example, is this an interdisciplinary volume for which I was invited to provide a 'legal' contribution? Might another contributor speak to the enslaved body in different (non-legal) terms? Might that cause me to take a more conservative approach to legal methodology than I might otherwise have done? Might another contributor speak to law and the racialised body in another context? (Jivraj, this volume) Are there synergies between different contributors? How far should I seek to draw them out or leave them to the reader and/or editors?

Beyond my contribution to the particular edited collection, I will also need to decide how my contribution might speak to existing debates and in which field. There is a huge literature on the body of the enslaved across a range of disciplines. I will need to decide if I wish primarily to add a distinctively legal perspective to some aspect of this literature or whether I seek to draw on non-legal literature to contribute to understanding law's relations with the body from a broader perspective. I will need to decide if I am writing a critical legal history or a contribution to the history of slaves and liberated Africans through their legal lives. It might be possible to do both of course. However, the opportunities (and limits) of my own disciplinary background would push me towards the former, even though I might also hope that my account might provide some useful analysis and legal detail for historians. Historian Suzanne

[1] For analysis of debates about the causes of abolition see, for example, Brown, 2006, pp. 15–16.

Schwarz, for example, has used the numerous lists of slaves and liberated Africans that the trade and its abolition generated to glean rich details about individuals' lives. When I first read such lists, the cursory descriptions of people and their bodies—typically height, sex and brief physical descriptions, including tattoos, scarification, injuries, branding marks, signs of illness and disease—I read absence, dislocation, trauma and objectification. The chilling phrase 'no marks', which I have seen repeated often, rang particularly hollow. Although Schwarz describes these registers as 'essentially bureaucratic listings of uprooted peoples caught in events beyond their control' (Schwarz, 2012, p 205), she also argues that '[t]he evidence contained in these early registers provides a basis for retrieving, at least in part, the life stories of displaced Africans from the anonymity imposed on them through the processes of enslavement and transportation' (Schwarz, 2012, p 179),[2] I am in awe of the work of scholars who read such records 'against the grain'.[3] Yet, in the end, I think it requires the work of historians or anthropologists. Here I come up against the limits of my own disciplinary capacity. In broad terms then, my focus is on a critical legal history.

The next question is how should I frame that contribution? My thinking about writing history has been profoundly influenced by the groundbreaking work of David Scott and the context or 'problem-space' he describes within which history is written (Scott, 2004, p 97). For my purposes, two approaches immediately present themselves, which offer different critical directions in the present. The first focuses on law's role in the commodification and racialisation of the body of the enslaved. The second emphasises resistance to this commodification. In the latter case, I might focus variously on resistance to law or resistance through law, or both, but either way I would seek to be alert to the resistance of enslaved and liberated Africans. In selecting between these different foci, I would consider the disciplinary skills I have to make each narrative 'stick', the narratives that might more naturally emerge from the archival sources consulted, as well as my own personal preferences. In reflecting on these choices here, I also seek to articulate some of the political choices that underpin the ways in which we might write a legal history of the body in the context of the transatlantic slave trade and abolition.

The Commodified and Racialised Body

My first thought would be to highlight the part law played in commodifying and racialising the body of enslaved individuals. Slavers violently trafficked a minimum of 12 million individuals to the Americas, of whom 10.5 million

[2] Schwarz is writing about the Registers of Liberated Africans in Sierra Leone which she uses alongside other records. Historian David Olusoga makes a similar argument, noting that the 'notion of the victims of the Atlantic trade as a great mass of de-individualized black humanity is suddenly and strikingly overthrown by the Registers of Liberated Africans' in Sierra Leone (Olusoga, 2016, p 313). See further, on registration and its use by historians, Engerman, 2012.

[3] On reading along and against the grain, see Stoler, 2002, 2009.

survived the Middle Passage (Walvin, 2007, p 448). Law played a key role in transforming the racialised body of the slave into property, resulting in a limited form of freedom even after abolition. Slaves were converted into 'an exchangeable unit' through 'legally binding documentary practices', including bills of lading (Rupprecht, 2016, p 34). Branded slaves' bodies were effectively trademarked to resist other claims of ownership (Johnson, 2016, p 231).[4] Maritime insurance benefitted slavers (Johnson, 2016, p 232)[5] until, at least in the British context, the Slave Trade Abolition Act 1807 prohibited insurances on slave trading. However, slave trade abolition did not end the commodification of liberated Africans' bodies. For one thing, the criss-crossing web of international treaties on slave trade repression still protected slavers' property rights in the bodies of those enslaved under certain circumstances in the early nineteenth century (Haslam, 2019). For another, liberated Africans were subject to 'various forms of coerced labor' (Lovejoy & Schwarz, 2015, p 21). Marcus Wood, for example, has described the British Abolition Act 1807 as 'a mean-spirited and highly efficient plan for the continued exploitation of the African body' (Wood, 2010, p 14). Moreover, the abolition of slavery in most parts of the British Empire in 1833 was dependent on providing compensation to slave owners for loss of property, and not to former slaves for their enslavement.[6] After the slave trade and slavery were abolished, liberated Africans and Asians were recruited as indentured labourers to the British West Indian colonies (Asiegbu, 1969, p 214; Mahmud, 2013). Indentured labourers continued to be insurable as human cargo (Lobban, 2007, p 328).[7] Law contributed to the creation of a racialised and commodified subject, and aspects of this framing persisted after abolition, albeit in a different guise. In these and other ways, scholars (Mahmud, 2013, p 228; Rupprecht, 2016, p 34) have shown how the creation of such subjects was inextricably linked to the rise of global capitalism.

There are many reasons for tracing the part law played in the construction of a racialised and commodified body, and much work, as the above shows, has been done. An account could serve as some form of narrative justice. It could be used to highlight ongoing effects of the slave trade and slavery and continuities in legal and economic structures that underpin the commodification of people today. It could foreground sites in which discussions about reparations—whether material or symbolic, individual or collective—might usefully

[4] Johnson cites Hugh Thomas as follows: 'Slaves of the Royal Africa Company were marked, with a burning iron upon the right breast, "DY", duke of York, after the chairman of the company': Johnson, 2016, p 232.

[5] One of the most well-known and horrific of such insurance cases is the *Zong* case. 130 sick and dying slaves were thrown overboard, the master reportedly having told the ship's crew that the owners would not be able to claim insurance in case of a 'natural death', in contrast to a situation where they were thrown overboard for the ship's safety. The first trial found the insurers were obliged to pay. A second trial was ordered but it did not determine the issue conclusively. *Gregson v Gilbert* 3 Doubl 232, 99 Eng Rep 629. See further, Lobban, 2007; and Oldham, 2007.

[6] See further, on compensation, Hall et al., 2015.

[7] Lobban is discussing an 1853 case, *Naylor v Palmer* concerning Chinese indentured labourers travelling to Peru.

take place.[8] It could also highlight the limitations of legal emancipation when it is unaccompanied by a contextual interrogation of legal processes including their material justice outcomes. More broadly, it might contribute to understanding, in the words of Mahmud, 'the relationship of modern law with capitalism and the global distributions of power, bodies and spaces that this relationship has engendered' (Mahmud, 2013, p 243). The focus on capitalism might also lead one to reflect, as Aouragh observes, discussing the work of Du Bois, that 'shared exploitation means that the fate of white and black workers under capitalism is interconnected' (Aouragh, 2019, p 9). While there may be particular political purchase in emphasising such social solidarity and cohesion, care must also be taken not to deny the distinctiveness of the racialised experience of slavery, or the experiences of racial discrimination today. Which of these—and potentially many other—framings is adopted will be influenced by the relevant audience to which the account is directed and the purpose it is to serve in the present. In other words, I would want to pay attention to the 'problem-space' (Scott, 2004, p 97) within which the account is written.

One concern is that emphasising the commodified and racialised body may come at the expense of an account which focuses on the agency and resistance of those enslaved. However, this is not inevitable. For example, in her exploration of the relationship between maritime insurance and the slave trade, Rupprecht explores how shipboard rebellions 'forced the question of whether a captured African—*en route* to his or her life of enslavement—could be the object of insurance and, if so, on what terms'. This was a question, she explains, that 'demanded an acknowledgement of human agency' (Rupprecht, 2016, p 42).

An account of law's role in the construction of a racialised and commodified slave body is vital to understanding the role of law in the slave trade and its contemporary legal legacies. However, my own particular interest lies in excavating the ways in which the resistance of enslaved individuals forced a confrontation with law and the resulting impact of such confrontation on legal development. I have a long-standing interest in the role of resistance in international law and in how law is navigated, resisted and subverted by those at its receiving end even, or especially where, such individuals are not accorded a formal role in its interpretation or development. Partly this derives from an interest in uncovering (alternative) stories, which is probably what drew me to the archive in the first place. Recognising unacknowledged contributors to legal change is also a matter of justice. By offering a richer understanding of how change occurs, and the effect of law on the ground, such approaches also provide a basis from which to analyse and, where necessary, rethink contemporary legal developments.

[8] See, for example, Rupprecht, 2016 on maritime insurance.

Agency and Resistance

Therefore, I might turn instead to explore enslaved people's resistance through or to law. While I would be concerned with how enslaved people's resistance impacted upon legal development, I would also be interested in resistance for its own sake. Acknowledging legal resistance can foreground contradictions inherent in specific legal forms. It can also act as a kind of memorialisation (see, further, Haslam, 2019, pp 17–18),[9] in a context in which there are limited opportunities to do justice to the immediate victims of the slave trade. Beyond doing justice to the past, what and how we memorialise about the past can contribute to shaping our legal focus, and the politics of recognition, in the present.

Focusing on legal resistance enables us to acknowledge the horrors of the slave trade and the remarkable capacity of individuals to survive it. My intention then would be to scour the case law for suggestions that slaves and liberated Africans took a more active role in challenging enslavement than a conventional legal account might suggest. This may be because they utilised the law to do so, or because their extra-legal confrontation provoked a legal challenge. For example, elsewhere I explore the actions of slaves on board two Brazilian slave ships, the *Activo* and *Perpetuo Defensor*, which had been captured by the British Navy. In line with slave trade repression treaties during the first part of the nineteenth century, these captured slave ships had been taken to Sierra Leone to one of the many Mixed Commissions established there. Mixed Commissions adjudicated the legality of the capture of certain slave ships and the fate of the slaves (or re-captives as they were also known) on board. However, while they were waiting for the Commission to adjudicate, the re-captives on board the *Activo* escaped to the shore. Those remaining on board the *Perpetuo Defensor* also resisted their continued detention with the result that the master of the ship felt forced to land them. Since, in the particular circumstances of these cases, the capture of both slave ships had taken place outside the strict provisions of the relevant slave trade repression treaty, it would have been expected that the re-captives would have been restored to those who were claiming ownership of them. Instead, however, after much legal wrangling, the re-captives were freed. I argued that it was their own actions, rather than the strict legal logic of the slave trade repression treaty, that ensured this (Haslam, 2019, pp 93–98). Building on this research, I would seek to draw upon, and to contribute to, accounts which challenge the omission of the agency of enslaved and liberated Africans from legal accounts of abolition (and to explore, where possible, their contribution to other areas of international law).[10]

[9] See further, on the idea of memorialisation, Douglas, 2011.

[10] For example, international legal orthodoxy typically traces the origins of modern human rights to the American and French declarations on the rights of men, not to the Haitian Revolution, although this framing is increasingly challenged.

To narrow further, I could, for example, focus on *habeas corpus* litigation. In focusing on *habeas corpus* litigation, I would be shifting my main inquiry from a commodified and racialised body to the body as a legal remedy. A fundamental remedy against illegal detention, *habeas corpus* literally requires the body to brought before the court. One concern is that a legal history of *habeas corpus* can easily slip into a congratulatory or progress narrative about legal and/or English freedom. This tendency is evident in some narratives about the famous test case concerning James Somerset which has played a dominant role in Anglo-American histories of abolition (*Somerset v Stewart* 1772).[11] One way to avoid this is to seek to write an account of *habeas corpus* from the perspective of the struggles of slaves themselves. For example, in the context of the United States, Lea VanderVelde has explored some 300 freedom suits filed by enslaved individuals in St. Louis (VanderVelde, 2014; see further, Brophy, 2017). I would be particularly interested in the ways in which enslaved individuals had a more active role in litigation than is evident from reading formal legal sources and/or the ways in which they contributed to the circumstances giving rise to *habeas corpus* applications in the first place.

The two narratives identified here (the commodified and racialised body, and resistance and *habeas corpus*) have different critical purchase and the second may be more fitting for the kind of archival work that animates me. In the end, the second narrative coincides with my more general interest in how individuals make sense of—and subvert—a legal world they were formally excluded from contributing to and how we might use counter-readings of cases to frame more widely accepted knowledge about cause and effect of legal change. However, there will still be some significant decisions to make.

Practical Concerns and the Politics of Knowledge Production

First, I would need to identify relevant (*habeas corpus*) cases. The potential legal 'archive' here is vast. The slave trade and abolition generated an enormous volume of legal documents, including litigation, both published and unpublished. I would need to make decisions about time periods and jurisdictions, and whether to focus on one or a series of cases. Since this is a potentially large project, for a contribution to an edited collection I might focus on one case. A close reading of one case could suit the nature of archival research. A single counter-reading of an already recognised leading case might become a starting point for a broader project. I might use a single starting point to help me to

[11] Although *Somerset*'s case is often taken to have abolished slavery in England, this interpretation, which was widely accepted at the time, is not borne out by a strict reading of the case in which Lord Mansfield only determined that it was illegal to transport slaves out of England against their will. Some of the myths around *Somerset* have centred on the phrase 'England is too pure an air for a slave to breathe in', which was in fact said by counsel, not the judge. For a counter-reading of this phrase, see Harris, 2006–2007. See further, Rabin, 2011.

hone a methodology with the intention of applying it more broadly. However, I might also approach the case with no such intention. Even so, it might spark a broader project, including by engaging my interest in themes and issues I had not otherwise thought of.

While there are well-discussed leading cases that took place within English courts, the temptation would be to go beyond these to explore *habeas corpus* applications elsewhere. I would expect that Sierra Leone, a colony set up for freed slaves and a central location for Britain's international abolition efforts, would be a fruitful starting point for research of this kind. However, I would need to consider what sources I can access within the time available. My experience of archival work is that it is slow, painstaking and often exhausting. This is more than matched by the regular excitement when an incident, phrase or event 'jumps off the page'. If I were to adopt a focus on Sierra Leone, I would need to trawl through colonial reports, letters between government departments, advice from the crown's law officers, records which are often handwritten, faded and sometimes only partly legible. This might be supplemented by the diaries of those involved in cases and news reports. If photography is allowed, I would obsessively photograph every potentially useful record whilst taking notes of the themes and ideas that each document suggests. An illegible document may be more easily read photographically on a bigger screen, and a photographic record enables me to return time and time again to the 'original' source and saves valuable note-taking time in the archive itself. I would annotate these notes later with the number of the photographic record. I would seek to read the legal case materials (whether published or unpublished) to explore the resistance of enslaved individuals and liberated Africans. Here critical approaches to the archive as explained below are so important because they challenge us to respond to silences in the legal sources, and legal sources are typically silent about, or only hint at, an active role on the part of those enslaved.

I would anticipate a number of challenges. First, archival research, like all research, is highly contingent, dependent on the vagaries of records having survived in the first place, having escaped official and unofficial destruction practices, and on legibility and reader fallibility, amongst others. Although my existing research has indicated that an examination *of habeas corpus* in this way could prove fruitful, there is always the possibility that one goes to the archive looking for one thing and ends up finding something different entirely, or that the archive does not 'speak' to what one is looking for. Practically, this means being alert to unexpected narratives.

Second, legal sources on slaves and liberated Africans are riven with silences. Writing legal history, especially about those whom the law and archival sources have silenced, is not simply a matter of adding silenced individuals to the legal record. Rather it requires choices to be made and articulated about the ways in which those individuals are written in. Here critical approaches to the archive are key. Critical approaches to the archive raise fundamental questions about silences in the (colonial) legal record for which critical reading practices are central. These reading practices can challenge silences and can suggest alternative narratives about what slaves' roles in *habeas corpus* litigation might have been. We recognise and act on the inherently political nature of history writing when we articulate these methods.

Third, there is inevitably a tension when adopting critical reading practices, such as reading 'against the grain', in being 'true' to the sources on the one hand and the political quest underpinning my research on the other, which is to write an account of *habeas corpus* which pays attention to the position and what might have been (since we cannot know) the perspective of enslaved individuals and liberated Africans. This underlying interest coincides with my long-standing legal and political interest in resistance and the ways that individuals and groups often in the direst circumstances make sense of and seek to shape the world around them. This tension can be reconciled to some extent by emphasising another kind of 'truth', one that centres on the silencing effects of law and legal records. Here then I would draw on Michel-Rolphe Trouillot's groundbreaking account of different types of silence in the context of the Haitian revolution. Trouillot encourages us to reflect upon different kinds of silences in history writing and what is at stake in each (Trouillot, 2015, p 26; see further Haslam, 2019, pp 16–17). Thus, I would need to identify and critique the silences while reading the legal case materials as well as to be alert to material that hints at the resistance of enslaved individuals and liberated Africans. Reading any case in this way provides a starting point to think through an alternative legal account, and to reflect on the assumptions underpinning orthodox understandings of legal change.

I would also need to make decisions about writing style. Should I use the term 'slave' or 'enslaved', 'slaver' or 'enslaver'? Should I use the term 'enslaved' when the legal sources refer to the term 'slave'? Do I need to make a decision about the slave's given or reported name(s), if there is one? Can I be sure to have picked up on the nuances of any nickname whether derogatory or otherwise? Beyond this, how to write about the body in the context of the transatlantic slave trade raises profound political and ethical dilemmas. Should I try to convey the tormented, detained or resisting body in a literary or more restrained legalistic style? Should I seek to emphasise or reconstruct and imagine the agony or let the facts speak for themselves? Is it possible for legal writing to convey what is so fundamentally unthinkable? Might an attempt to reconstruct the trauma risk reproducing what Saidiya Hartman has described as 'the hyper-embodiness of the powerless' (Hartman, 1997, p 19)? How is it possible to acknowledge the pain without creating in her words a 'spectacle of suffering' (ibid.)? Are any suggested alternative legal readings of cases more convincing and authoritative the more restrained my writing style remains? Might this depend on my audience? Here then I return to questions asked at the beginning: for whom am I writing and whom do I seek to persuade and of what? These questions are not, of course, unique to my project. For example, there is an important and rich literature on the representation of the holocaust (see famously, e.g. Adorno, 1955). I would need to decide whether I would draw on this literature in order to think through these questions, or whether I would remain focused on literature on the representation of the slave trade. These decisions are both principled (is it possible to apply literature from one context to another without losing the specificity of each?) and practical (how much space and time is there to do justice to, and incorporate, another body of research?).

To the extent I would resolve these dilemmas of representation, it would be by consciously articulating my choices, while acknowledging their pitfalls and the promises of the options and alternatives I reject. In the end, I think I would heed the above warning about the description and re-inscription of bodily suffering. While I would wish to emphasise law's complicity in the horrors of slavery and the slave trade, my concern would be that a poorly executed attempt to encapsulate such terrors through a more literary style would (in my case) risk appropriating the bodies of those enslaved and would be better left to those who can do them justice (see, e.g. Morrison, 1987; Philip, 2008).

Conclusion

If I were asked to contribute to an edited collection on the body, my starting point would be to reflect upon the role of law in the commodification of enslaved individuals' bodies. I would wish to explore how enslaved individuals and liberated Africans resisted commodification both through and against law in the context of the transatlantic slave trade and abolition.

Legal accounts inevitably provide only a partial view. While my focus on law results from my disciplinary training and my interest in the legal world, litigation can offer glimpses into individuals' lives and some of the structures that constrained them (Haslam, 2019, p 19). Litigation can also show how some individuals were able to contest, subvert and/or to contribute to changing those structures. This contribution has focused on the ultimately politically infused choices that I would need to make. History writing is never neutral. However, the choices involved in writing a legal history of the transatlantic slave trade feel particularly significant because of its enormity and its continuing consequences in the present.[12] Whilst these continuing effects lend urgency to the research and writing, they also lend complexity. Complexity stems from an awareness of the limitations deriving from my own disciplinary positioning and the multiple ways in which these narratives might have political purchase in the present. I have identified two possible approaches I might feasibly take. One is to focus on the role of law in constructing a commodified and racialised body. The other looks at the body more indirectly by exploring challenges to the slave trade and slavery through the legal device of *habeas corpus*. These

[12] See further, for example, on the continuing consequences of the slavery and the slave trade, the website of the CARICOM Reparations Commission: 'Ever since slavery was abolished in the Caribbean … and in the broader Americas … the victims of slavery and their progeny have been struggling for justice to repair the damages wrought by this most horrific of crimes against humanity.' CARICOM Reparations Commission at https://caricomreparations.org accessed 26 August 2021.

approaches and sites are, of course, by no means all-encompassing or exclusive. Which I might select would depend upon a number of factors, including who I am writing for alongside the resources at my disposal; my disciplinary limitations and personal partialities, as well as how I envisage this history feeds into contemporary pre-occupations. The decision to focus on *habeas corpus* rather than a more flesh-and-blood memorialisation of the body of the slave represents an erasure of sorts. However, I would hope that it would facilitate an account which would emphasise the resistance and agency of enslaved and liberated Africans and centre it in a narrative about the development of *habeas corpus*, which has been and remains a central tool to challenge unlawful detention.

References

Adorno, T. W. (1955). *Prismen: Kulturkritik und Gesellschaft*. Suhrkamp.

Aouragh, M. (2019). "White Privilege" and Shortcuts to Anti-racism. *Race and Class, 61*(2), 3–26.

Asiegbu, J. U. J. (1969). *Slavery and the Politics of Liberation 1787–1861*. Longman.

Brophy, A. L. (2017). Slaves as Plaintiffs. *Michigan Law Review, 15*(6), 895–914.

Brown, C. L. (2006). *Moral Capital: Foundations of British Abolitionism*. North Carolina Press.

Douglas, S. (2011). Between Constitutional Mo(nu)ments: Memorialising Past, Present and Future and the District Six Museum and Constitution Hill. *Law and Critique, 22*, 171–187.

Engerman, S. L. (2012). Monitoring the Abolition of the International Slave Trade: Slave Registration in the British Caribbean. In K. Breckenridge & S. Szreter (Eds.), *Registration and Recognition: Documenting the Person in World History*. Oxford University Press.

Hall, C., Draper, N., McClelland, K., Donnington, K., & Lang, R. (2015). *Legacies of British Slave Ownership: Colonial Slavery and the Formation of Victorian Britain*. Cambridge University Press.

Hamilton, K., & Shaikh, F. (2012). Introduction. In K. Hamilton & P. Salmon (Eds.), *Slavery, Diplomacy and Empire: Britain and the Suppression of the Slave Trade, 1807–1975*. Sussex Academic Press.

Harris, C. (2006–2007). "Too Pure an Air": Somerset's Legacy from Anti-slavery to Colorblindness. *Texas Wesleyan Law Review, 13*, 439–458.

Hartman, S. (1997). *Scenes of Subjection: Terror, Slavery and Self-Making in Nineteenth-Century America*. Oxford University Press.

Haslam, E. (2019). *The Slave Trade, Abolition and the Long History of International Criminal Law: The Recaptive and the Victim*. Routledge.

Johnson, S. (2016). Branded: Trademarks Tattoos, Slave Owner Brands, and the Right to Have "Free" Skin. *Michigan Telecommunications and Technology Law Review, 22*(2), 225–269.

Lobban, M. (2007). Slavery, Insurance and the Law. *Journal of Legal History, 28*(3), 319–328.

Lovejoy, P. E., & Schwarz, S. (2015). Sierra Leone in the Eighteenth and Nineteenth Centuries. In P. E. Lovejoy & S. Schwarz (Eds.), *Slavery, Abolition and the Transition to Colonialism in Sierra Leone*. Africa World Press.

Mahmud, T. (2013). Cheaper than a Slave: Indentured Labor, Colonialism, and Capitalism. *Whitter Law Review, 23*, 215–244.

Mawani, R. (2012). Law's Archive. *Annual Review of Law and Society Science, 8*, 337–365.

Morrison, T. (1987). *Beloved*. Alfred A Knopf.

Oldham, J. (2007). Insurance Litigation Involving the *Zong* and Other British Slave Ships, 1780–1807. *Journal of Legal History, 28*(3), 299–318.

Olusoga, D. (2016). *Black and British: A Forgotten History*. Macmillan.

Philip, M. N. (2008). *Zong! As told to the author by Setaey Adamu Boateng* Weslyan University Press.

Rabin, D. (2011). 'In a Country of Liberty?': Slavery, Villeinage and the Making of Whiteness in the Somerset Case (1772). *History Workshop Journal, 72*, 5–29.

Rupprecht, A. (2016). "Inherent Vice": Marine Insurance, Slave Ship Rebellion and the Law. *Race and Class, 57*(3), 31–44.

Schwarz, S. (2012). Reconstructing the Life Histories of Liberated Africans: Sierra Leone in the Early Nineteenth Century. *History in Africa, 39*, 175–207.

Scott, D. (2004). *Conscripts of Modernity: The Tragedy of Colonial Enlightenment*. Duke University Press.

Sherwood, M. (2007). *After Abolition: Britain and the Slave Trade Since 1807*. IB Tauris.

Stoler, A. (2002). Colonial Archives and the Arts of Governance. *Archival Science, 2*, 87–109.

Stoler, A. (2009). *Along the Archival Grain: Epistemic Anxieties and Colonial Common Sense*. Princeton University Press.

Trouillot, M.-R. (2015). *Silencing the Past Power and the Production of History*. Beacon Press.

VanderVelde, L. (2014). *Redemption Songs: Suing for Freedom before Dred Scott*. Oxford University Press.

Walvin, J. (2007). Slave Trade. In D. Dabydeen, J. Gilmore, & C. Jones (Eds.), *The Oxford Companion to Black British History*. Oxford University Press.

Wood, M. (2010). *The Horrible Gift of Freedom Atlantic Slavery and the Representation of Emancipation*. University of Georgia Press.

Cases

Gregson v Gilbert 3 Doubl 232; 99 Eng Rep 629.

Naylor v Palmer (1853) 8 Exch 739.

Somerset v Stewart (1772) Lofft 1, 98 Eng Rep 499 (KB 1772).

CHAPTER 3

Bodies, Medicine and Otherness

Emilie Cloatre

Abstract In this chapter, I explore how I would approach the hypothetical exercise of writing a chapter for a book on 'Law and the Body'. As a socio-legal scholar whose work is mostly on issues of law and medicine, the theme of the book would echo quite closely much of the focus of my work. Yet, I have not to date engaged as explicitly with the body as such a specific invitation would require. As a result, the exercise would be one of thinking through a new lens about my ongoing research, and empirical data, and engaging both familiar and less familiar questions and resources. In this piece, I try to chart what the process and its outcome may look like, proposing that my focus would be on a particular series of empirical questions that have emerged as I researched the regulation of traditional healing in Senegal.

Keywords Traditional healing • Medicine • Medical anthropology • Senegal • STS • Socio-legal

Introduction

My research mainly focuses on the interface between law and medicine: writing a paper on bodies would therefore be fitting. Even though I tend to identify primarily as a socio-legal scholar, I engage almost as heavily with other disciplines in which bodies occupy a central place (medical anthropology and sociology, global health, and, to a more minor extent, the history of medicine). Yet, thinking about bodies (or indeed making my research speak to this

E. Cloatre (✉)
University of Kent, Canterbury, UK
e-mail: e.cloatre@kent.ac.uk

D. Herman, C. Parsley (eds.), *Interdisciplinarities*, Palgrave Socio-Legal Studies, https://doi.org/10.1007/978-3-030-89297-5_3

particular thematic) has been less central to my work than engaging with the knowledges, institutions, and relationships that underpin the practice of medicine(s) and its regulation. Writing a chapter explicitly about bodies and law would invite me to approach my research from a new angle, or at least with a different emphasis. Like most interdisciplinary scholars, how I approach such an invitation would depend on the particular audience I am addressing, and the other contributions to the volume. For the purpose of 'thinking through', I will chart here what would be my approach to a volume in which scholars are invited to specifically unpick the relationship between bodies and law across thematic fields, and where the intended audience has a particular interest and expertise in law.

Law, Medicine, and the Body

Even though most of my writing is based on empirical work, as I commence, I usually approach the exercise of writing with a broader context in mind. The work I sketch out below, for example, fits into a more general set of questions relating to the interface between law and medicine and their relationship to the body. Regulations, both within medical law and beyond, contribute to hindering or facilitating the making of 'healthy bodies'. However, the ways in which the translation from legal rules to everyday practice happens often escape the attention of regulators, as those constrained by such rules use their imagination to redefine the form and boundaries of their practice. At the same time, the making of regulations that surround medicine involves complex choreographies where scientific knowledge (or what counts as such) gets translated into political and legal choices and regulatory decision-making. In these processes, everyday health practices, themselves rooted in institutional and cultural histories, come to reshape how legal regulations are implemented, challenged, evaded or reimagined. In many ways, these questions provide fertile insights into broader societal patterns that my research tries to unpack. These processes also lend themselves to empirical inquiries in order to unearth some of the minute ways into which translations and transformations happen in everyday practice.

To approach a chapter on 'law and the body', and because the theme is so close to my own work, I would build on my existing (or ongoing) data to speak to the thematics of the book. At the moment, my main project explores how different legal systems regulate what we may label as 'alternative/complementary' or 'traditional' medicines—in effect, practices and therapies that differ from biomedical paradigms in some fundamental way and often sit on the edge of the main state-sanctioned systems of healthcare.[1] This is a topic that has been of interest to me both because of the intrinsic challenges it raises and because of the broader phenomena that it can bring to mind. Healing systems have long and messy histories, and their place in healthcare has been shaped by

[1] This project is supported by the Wellcome Trust [grant 200380/Z/15/Z].

the emergence of state medicine and the legalisation of some types of techniques, of training, and of materials rather than others (Ramsey, 1999; Wahlberg, 2007; Langwick, 2011). Law is and has always been central to delimiting the boundaries of legitimate healthcare: from the regulation of professions to that of materials, to the determination of where interventions over the body may be considered as tolerable for the purpose of healing, and where they should be considered as only harmful, law plays a central role in establishing the formal boundaries of practice. Healing practices, however, are also deeply rooted in societal configurations: scholars have long pointed to the gendered and racialised tensions that animate biomedicine, and decisions over how other forms of healings are legitimised or delegitimised echo these questions (Vaughan, 1991; Adams, 2002; Ehrenreich & English, 2010). Traditions in healing are also deeply cultural and build on long histories of local tensions within populations, or superimposed over them, maybe most strikingly so in the colonial and postcolonial context (Wahlberg, 2006; Bivins, 2010; Vasconi, 2016). The question of how practices that sit on the edge of medicine should be regulated therefore speaks to much broader phenomena: what (and whose) knowledge matters for the purpose of regulation, how do different regulatory and medical systems deal with those who dissent, and what kind of effects does the interface between biomedical and legal institutions have on other healing (and cultural) practices?

Unpacking how healing paradigms are accounted for in law and policy—and exploring how lines are drawn between those that are supported, those that are simply tolerated, and those that are more actively considered illegal and/or illegitimate—also raises fundamental questions about how states choose to balance societal and personal freedoms in healing (and often, in beliefs) and the universal claims of medical science (Cloatre, 2019). They also highlight the challenges of determining how to prove efficacy for medical and regulatory science: if clear paths have been established to determine if pharmaceuticals or vaccines work (even if they may remain contested), these are more blurry when healing relies on less standardised or measurable entities (such as raw plants) (Urquiza Haas & Cloatre, 2021). Those who see incantations as part of their healing process, or believe that the relationship between healer and patient is central to the act of healing, will face yet more robust obstacles in seeking to prove that the practice they embrace 'works' (Adams, 2002). The reliance of biomedicine on the assumption that minds and bodies are separate spheres of existence and that ways of healing need to be proven through bodily evidence has been largely embraced by regulatory logics. Yet, numerous healing practices continue to rely on a very different cosmology and a different bodily ontology. Even where laws do not explicitly privilege one type of ontology over others, the powers given to biomedical institutions to police the boundaries of healing practices may have similar effects.

Making sense of how various healing practices coexist with biomedicine, and how they are influenced by specific regulations and legal systems (in a more generic sense), therefore speaks to how law accommodates different cultural understandings of how bodies function (as materials). In my own work, I approach these questions through interdisciplinary methods at the crossroad of law and the social sciences, building in particular on some of the key questions that Science and Technology Studies (STS) engage in relation to the making of scientific (and other) knowledge and its social construction. In approaching a particular chapter or piece of writing, I might take much of this for granted, yet it underpins my particular interest in the production of knowledge and its expression through social relations and institutions, and indeed its effects on social inequalities, which is particularly striking in the context of biomedicine. As I approach the chapter sketched out below, this broader picture and particular standpoints would frame my thinking, shaping both what I am likely to consider would be an interesting topic to share with others, but also the kind of issues that I am most likely to pick up—or indeed produce—through my data.

Methodology: What Story to Tell?

The chapter I would be writing on the body would build onto the stories that my project on law and alternative/traditional medicines has produced so far. This project, like much of my previous work, relies on qualitative research methods. It is also built on a series of case studies, in Western Europe (France and England), West Africa (Ghana and Senegal) and the West Indian Ocean (Mauritius and La Réunion): rather than imagining these as purely comparative, my approach is rooted in the assumption that research—empirical or otherwise—can only provide particular snapshots of much broader and multiple realities. In this project, none of these case studies is expected to give a complete and definite picture of what law means for traditional medicine, or vice versa. Instead, I am interested in juxtaposing snapshots in order to illustrate some of the frictions that arise when states seek to regulate alternative and/or traditional healing. While some of these are constant across case studies (e.g. the difficulty of creating regulatory order when the tests and logics of science do not map onto the ontological and epistemological claims being made), others are the result of social and cultural particularities.

Given the scale of the project and of the data that it has produced, a chapter on the body could build on almost any case study, as well as cut across them to produce a more general and maybe more conceptual overview of what looking at law and traditional medicine as a global set of relationships can suggest in terms of questions of rights over both sick and healthy bodies. This would be one of the first choices to be made upon receiving the invitation, and a translation of a general 'what do I want to write about/what do I have to say about this' question. It would determine the balance between empirical nitty-gritty details and conceptual framing, but would also need to account for the audience: if the detailed history or social experience of a particular healing practice, or particular healing bodies, in relation to regulation might be of interest to those who work on similar topics in medical anthropology or sociology, legal scholars may find it more pertinent to think about how the area can help us continue to make sense of the type of social practice that we label 'legal' and its embodied translations. Inevitably, the final choices would also be about timings and may be slightly opportunistic: which set of data I am most embedded in at a particular time might determine which story I end up deciding to tell.

Because I am currently working on data from Senegal, if I were invited to write a chapter on the body today, it is likely that I would focus my chapter on how broader questions from the project are playing out in this particular context, and particularly on how the boundaries of legal healing are defined. One particular puzzle I may focus the chapter on is how the work done by legal and biomedical institutions comes to construct particular lines of tolerance, whereby healers are tolerated only insofar as their practice does not look too much like biomedicine, yet, at the same time, are expected to demonstrate the scientific rationality of their work. I return to this in some detail below, but first I set out the more general picture that makes this specific focus pertinent—or at least the most obvious direction in which to take the proposed chapter. Thinking through the policing that takes place over healing in Senegal, and who gets to determine how traditional healers can interact with bodies while remaining within the sphere of legal healing, would be an example of the kind of snapshot that I hoped to obtain through my case studies, echoing broader questions around how legal and biomedical institutions jointly shape the boundaries of healing, while at the same time reflecting the socio-historical particularities of Senegalese health practices and health governance.

The chapter, as is the case for each of the case studies in my project, would build on in-depth interviews, some observation, and documentary materials. Data collection was a collective endeavour, and I have benefited from the support of a team of researchers in carrying out this work, particularly since the Covid crisis made international travel impossible. As a result, the proposed chapter would almost definitely be co-authored: the ideas I am sketching here would be my proposal to colleagues, and the final chapter would inevitably be reshaped by our collective conversations. The data on which we would build aimed to try to understand debates both from the top down (how governments and regulators have approached alternative and traditional medicine) and from the bottom-up (how actors who practise and/or promote alternative and/or traditional medicine have engaged with state regulation, and what normativities they have deployed alongside it to order their own practice). At the same time, the analysis aims to place this empirical material in its historical and social context, trying to make sense of the ways in which practices (both of regulation and of healing) have evolved over the years, including how colonial histories have influenced contemporary relations.

If part of the process of data collection has been to unearth some factual information—such as legal texts, formal statements by institutions, official positions of individuals or organisations—it has been, maybe more crucially, about documenting perspectives and experiences. This latter subjective dimension of qualitative research is both its limitation and what makes it, in my view, most valuable: there is no escaping the fact that what emerges are always partial stories, shaped by the particular voices of others, and this impacts the writing process to follow. The story is never complete and inevitably always limited to those voices that were heard. Truths are contested, and even what might be taken as a 'factual' starting point usually unravels as it is contextualised and commented upon. Accumulating further data might bring resolution on some matters, but for most others this fluid nature is the effect of the multiplicity of the social world itself on which one singular story can never be superimposed. Even with those limitations, however, empirical work is what puts flesh into (at least my own) understandings of how law operates in everyday lives, and what kind of visions it fosters, acknowledges, or seeks to supersede.

As I start planning the chapter, I would begin by thinking about how to segment the stories that have emerged from empirical data and reflect on whether they speak to the particular theme of the book. But the process also works the other way: starting with a specific focus on bodies in mind would shape how I approached the data, nudging me to pay attention to statements or phrasings that may not have jumped out otherwise. Writing and analysing are inevitably co-productive.

Conceptualising Data

At the same time, contextualising and making sense of data requires a thorough engagement with other scholarly works. This is also what will make a particular piece relevant to a broader audience. In general, my work is in close conversation with thematic literature that has engaged with alternative and traditional medicines as socio-cultural phenomena. For the proposed chapter, I would want to start by charting the key contributions from this scholarship that I build upon, before reflecting on what the particular stories from Senegal might add to what others have already explored. Traditional medicine is a very long-standing focus of sociological, anthropological, and historical work. Yet, law itself has rarely been the focus of this work, and the interaction of healing and legalities (and indeed their co-production) remains understudied. This affects both the audiences I would aim to speak to and the kind of work I could most productively build upon. My chapter would aim to address both a legal audience who may not have any particular interest in traditional medicine per se, but might find the broader questions around knowledge-making, regulations and institutions relevant, and an interdisciplinary audience of scholars with expertise in medical pluralism for whom thinking about how legal processes fit into the broader social processes at play may be of interest. At the same time, my chapter would build upon the work of others who have explored in depth the knowledge systems upon which different kinds of healing rest and, indeed, their understandings of the body and how those have been transformed, rewritten, reinvented, and/or preserved over the years (Fassin & Fassin, 1988; Langwick, 2006, 2011; Osseo-Asare, 2014). It would also build on socio-legal scholarship, and in particular work that has interrogated the making of legalities through everyday practices, including through legal consciousness scholarship and anthropological explorations of legal relationships (e.g. Ewick & Silbey, 1998; Mezey, 2001; Silbey, 2005).

This would provide some of the basic conceptual background for thinking through a particular story from Senegal that has intrigued me. Senegal, like many other African states, has a long history of medical pluralism: traditional practices vary across regions, overlap with religious traditions, and coexist with a biomedical system that is more accessible to some than to others. Traditional healing has not, to date, been explicitly regulated by the state, although a much-debated Bill is attempting to do just this at the moment. Given the opposition it has attracted from several circles, including the Ordre des Médecins, it is not clear, however, whether it will ever be successfully adopted. At the same time, traditional medicine is impacted by the law on illegal medical practice, a 1966 law, adopted on the model of previous colonial legislation, which organises the conditions of practice of medicine. One of the conditions it sets is that, to practise medicine legally, one must have a medical degree and be registered with the Ordre des Médecins. Anyone who carries out a medical act without meeting these conditions would be committing the criminal offence of 'exercice illégal de la médecine'. This is not to say that anyone doing 'healing' is doing so illegally: much hinges on the contentious definition of what constitutes a medical act. To a large extent, this definition has been left to the professional associations of biomedical practitioners—the Ordre des Médecins in particular—who tend to be the groups initiating complaints and denunciations that lead to the occasional prosecution of healers. A certain tolerance towards traditional healing, together with an understanding that traditional healers operate in a different sphere to that of biomedicine, means that many traditional healers never cross the boundary that would bring them to court. But, occasionally, those boundaries are crossed, and the Ordre des Médecins decides to intervene. In our interviews, one such boundary came up repeatedly and could form the starting point of my proposed chapter. Some contemporary healers, keen to use all the resources they can to diagnose their patients, occasionally send them out to undertake biomedical tests—X-rays, blood tests, ultrasounds, and so on. They ask their patient to return with the results of the test so that they can then proceed to offer traditional remedies. For the Ordre des Médecins, this is a clear infringement into the territory of biomedicine and one scenario in which the law on illegal medical practice is relevant, and this is a common ground for initiating legal procedures. Healers are aware of and have adapted to such risk: they are cautious in suggesting rather than prescribing medical tests, often ask patients to write down details of the test to be requested, rather than write it themselves (so that it is harder to claim that the test was 'prescribed' by the healer), and overall try to avoid being seen as the ones to initiate a demand for diagnostic test. A careful choreography ensues, where practitioners operate along very fragile lines of legality and legitimacy, and the law itself becomes translated through a tacit form of everyday negotiation.

There is much in this seemingly simple story that I would like to unpack. Some of the practices at stake echo what others have demonstrated of the difficulty of defining 'traditional' healing, as traditional healers often borrow techniques and tools from a range of knowledge systems, transforming and reinventing themselves to fit the needs and opportunities of particular times (Hampshire & Asiedu Owusu, 2013; Pordié & Gaudillère, 2013). Interactions between traditional medicine and biomedicine also fluctuate—overlapping occasionally as here—while also creating new frictions. Here, these relationships become complicated by the pre-existence of legal tools that effectively enable biomedical institutions to monitor the boundaries of their professional monopoly, delimiting what they consider as being unacceptable intrusions and, in that process, framing the possibilities that are open to other traditions. In the context of Senegal, as in others, this particular use of the law also finds its roots in colonial histories: even if the 1966 law is particular in its phrasing and application to Senegal, its roots are in French law and its import during the colonial period. Similarly, the current structure of the Ordre des Médecins is in part a legacy of the colonial era. This also fits into much broader historical relations between agents of colonial states and local healers, and between local populations and colonial doctors, that constitutes an important background to understanding any question surrounding the governance of healing, as well as patterns of resistance, avoidance or engagement with state law, and indeed the importance of defining legally what different agents can and cannot do (and who gets to draw those lines). More than an abstract set of encounters between 'biomedicine' and traditional healers, the legal boundary-setting that takes place in Senegal is about institutional power and the significance of the Ordre des Médecins in determining what is acceptable or not.

I would also want to reflect on why tools of diagnosis are a particularly contentious issue. Usually, such boundary-setting by biomedical institutions hinges on notions of risk, for example, when products are given as treatment by unqualified practitioners. This is less explicit in this case, where the concern is arguably over an act of 'knowing' rather than 'doing'. At the same time, a fear often attached to non-biomedical healing is that patients who turn to alternative or traditional healing are driven away from biomedicine itself: arguably, this turn to biomedical diagnostic tools could be a way to facilitate the interface between two systems between which patients navigate. Tentatively, it seems that the concern at stake is one of blurring the boundaries between what should (at least for the Ordre des Médecins) remain clearly distinct systems, with different ways of both diagnosing bodies and ultimately treating them. Letting traditional healers use diagnostic tools suggests an intrusion onto the epistemological resources of biomedicine and the expression of a different kind of knowledge over the body which makes them potentially more problematic in the eyes of biomedical institutions.

In order to make sense of this, I would need to return to other analyses of the interactions between biomedicine and traditional healing, with a view to interrogating the kind of conditions that need to be placed upon traditional healing in order to make it 'tolerable' for biomedical institutions. Returning to the empirical data from Senegal would also give me a more detailed reading of how different actors seem to frame this particular issue. Yet, neither scholarly analyses from other contexts nor empirical data will give definite answers as to why this particular issue has become a sticky point in the application of the law, and one where illegal medical practice affects traditional healing. The reading I would be proposing would inevitably carry a degree of interpretation, grounded on multiple resources to try to make sense of the stakes of a particular debate.

Thinking About Law

As I think through these issues, I would also keep in mind broader questions about law—its nature and modes of action and what it can be seen to do in this particular story, which ultimately are always part of the puzzles I want to engage with. Essentially, the story at stake here is one of the interactions between law and particular knowledges and their mediation through institutional arrangements. At their core, legal decisions about which healing practices are considered as legitimate or not tend to build onto claims over the rationality of different kinds of knowledge systems. But the relationships between law and alternative or traditional healing also rests on multiple legal orders that not only become articulated in the everyday practice of healing, but also on the expression of law through very particular institutional translations of its principles: here, the Ordre des Médecins is a key source of influence in determining when the law should be triggered and how it should be mobilised. This is not uncommon and illustrates the often symbiotic relationship between law and biomedicine (and its institutions).

At the same time, other healers' relationship to formal state law is fragile. This requires healers to operate their own systems to determine what behaviours are acceptable or not and to adjust their practices to avoid having to encounter the force of the law, in both individual and collective ways, sharing experiences and learning from others' practices to limit their own precarity. This is not unique to this example, and forms of self-regulation are present in many of the practices that my project has considered. Such systems are never entirely cut-off from the law, sometimes acting 'instead of' state law, creating alternative systems to triage legitimate or non-legitimate healers, sometimes laying the groundings for future claims to be authorised or regulated. In the case of Senegalese healers and their use of diagnostic tools from biomedicine, practices are adjusted in response to a particular interpretation of the law. Legal effects go through a number of loops, travelling through the interpretation of biomedical doctors, back to prosecutors and courts, and back to individual healers themselves who adapt to ongoing pressures.

In this latter movement, the story of healers in Senegal also gives a snapshot of a broader concern that cuts across each of my case studies, speaking to the question of how those who sit on the edge of legality respond to the law and its interpretation. In Senegal, traditional healers have not received formal recognition by the state, in the way they have in neighbouring countries. Yet, there, as in other contexts where healers have not received legal backing, they tend to engage with the law, at least to some degree. The choreographies that healers devise to continue to use biomedical diagnostic tools while remaining under the radar of the Ordre des Médecins are part of a broader picture of coexisting with the law and the everyday tactics that limit their legal precarity. In these processes, healing practices themselves are affected: healing techniques are adjusted, professions reinvented and interactions redefined so that frictions with the formal legal system remain limited. This happens alongside ongoing negotiations for legal recognition, which matters more to some healers than others, and is also only seen as acceptable if it does not involve yet further oversight from biomedical doctors. One of the key stakes of legal recognition is the extent to which the acceptance of alternative ontologies by a legal system that has closely operated with and through biomedical institutions would require further taming and transformation. When drafting the chapter, I would need to think carefully about where to draw boundaries around the story, and whether the story of how illegal medical practice is enacted in particular ways can be told without also engaging broader questions around the negotiation of legal status for traditional healers.

As far as analytical resources are concerned, and to make sense in particular of the stories of law at stake, I would start by reaching out to STS-inflected work that has drawn on ideas of relationality and materiality to approach the messiness of everyday social practices (Latour & Porter, 1993; Law & Mol, 1995; Mol, 2003). This is the main theoretical tradition that I have relied upon in my work to date and where my expertise lies. Like for most scholars, this is in part the effect of my own training and 'where I come from' academically, and it continues to influence how I approach particular matters. At the same time, those perspectives echo how I tend to see the world and the type of puzzles that I want to think through in my work—micro-practices through which much can be learned about how social relations operate. This is also the set of perspectives that I started from when designing my current projects, and that have quietly shaped, in the background, the type of questions, type of literatures and types of networks I have attached the project to. For the same reasons, STS work would also be my starting point to think about the making—and policing—of knowledge and the role of particular institutions in producing and maintaining power over knowledge (Bora, 2008; Epstein, 1996; Jasanoff, 2006). Of course, legal relations themselves are rarely at the core of STS research, so, although the methodological tools help me decentre and 'flatten out' the legal as part of broader social relationships, I build onto more explicitly 'legal' scholarship to reflect on what my data suggests about our more general understanding of law. Thinking about the practice of coexisting with the law as an 'everyday' experience, which has emerged from much of the data on which I would build, echoes concerns cutting across legal anthropology, in particular those related to 'legal consciousness' and the law of the everyday, as well as scholarship on everyday illegality (Roitman et al., 2006; De Genova, 2013; Cloatre & Enright, 2017). In addition, underlying much of the tensions at stake between doctors and healers is the question of otherness, and what kind of otherness is tolerated: here, it is a form of otherness that seems tolerable only as long as it remains within its own sphere, without tentatively crossing boundaries of knowing. Both feminist and postcolonial scholarship on science and the patterns of uneven power that organise relationships between states and scientific institutions would provide some pointers towards the making of such boundaries of legitimacy across law and (bio)medicine (Harding, 1991, 1998; Haraway, 1994, 2007). Finally, because the particular story I would like to explore is so centrally about institutions, the decentralisation of mechanisms of legal governance and the interface between socio-political power and biomedical knowledge, it may be that I would need to venture into the less familiar (to me) territory of governmentality and biopolitics. But I would very much see each of these engagements as being at least in part about making sense of the empirical story.

Writing

The process of writing the chapter itself would involve huge amounts of back and forth, between data and literature, and indeed many drafts and iteration. I find writing—and writing from data in particular—a difficult process: drawing the boundaries of the story, deciding which details to give and which may just be tedious to the reader, what to foreground and when, how much background to give, these choices always create infinite dilemmas. Writing a chapter for a thematic edited collection, rather than a standalone paper, also has its own challenges: here, focusing on bodies as a starting point, rather than what tend to be my more familiar 'starting points' (healers, healing practices, or materials such as medicinal plants) will require some rethinking of both data and literature in some of the ways I have suggested. Indeed, in the story I have presented here, bodies may still be more discrete than they would need to be to echo the particular focus of the book. Writing from data has its practical challenges—not only in terms of if and how to use direct quotes or not, how much theorising to do with the raw data itself, but also how to 'do justice' to the stories offered by informants. Writing about activities that are 'technically illegal' brings its own challenges, including in striking the difficult balance between describing and seemingly denouncing. In writing about these issues, my main aim is to convey perspectives and frictions, rather than polemics: ultimately, my work is not about whose understanding of the body is 'correct' (though in this sensitive field one is always aware that words can be interpreted to fit other agendas).

Writing in this field is also complicated by an ethical awareness of some of the abuses that have permeated healing over the years, reflected in each of our case studies that go beyond ontological tensions, and break away from a common sense of ethics that is not exclusive to biomedicine. If regulating healing practices is often centred on how to 'catch' abusive practices in the net of law, my work is concerned with all the other things that such legal strategies do, and the excesses in Othering that they produce. Engaging with these excesses, and those who challenge them, while remaining aware of the possibility of risk and abuse that needs to be also accounted for, requires careful writing. Often, however, those whom I have met in my research address these questions in their own words: they are aware of the risk that the field of healing creates and are keen to draw boundaries. Yet, they also want to propose alternative means of thinking of bodies and the act of healing in ways that are not limited to the perspective of biomedicine. They suggest approaches that are often not only about knowledge but also about politics. In Senegal, as elsewhere, healers and their users confront the state with some powerful questions about how we treat bodies, in every sense of the word. They are also agents who operate, regardless of what the law will do, and develop their own sense of ethics. Yet, they remain aware that some practices use similar discourses to propose something very different and potentially more abusive: stories of healers that have exhorted vast amounts of money, injured or physically abused patients, are also part of the field and those individuals risk discrediting the others. What makes the regulation of this field difficult also makes writing about it challenging: any sentence that recognises the multiplicity of healing ontologies (not only in Senegal but also, for example, in the contexts of France or England when talking about alternative healing) and the bodily ontologies underlying them could also be misconstrued as supporting the wildest claims that the most caricatural 'quacks' would make. This is, of course, one of the challenges of STS work in general: acknowledging the limitations of science as a provider of unique truth and rationality can easily be misconstrued as claiming that anything goes.

In addition to all these challenges, the act of writing itself is unpredictable. No matter how neat an idea may initially seem, it can get messy as it unravels: in my career to date, the papers that took longest to come together are not the ones that I had initially thought would prove most difficult, and vice versa. Usually, having a clear sense of what story a chapter will tell, or having in mind a particular empirical story that will anchor the chapter, tends to make the process easier. But I have found myself drowning in a fast-unravelling narrative too many times to ever approach the process of writing with calmness nor confidence.

Finally, the process I have focused on assumes a certain degree of abstraction. I have left aside the kind of practical questions and challenges that, in real-life academia, often complicate the processes of publishing and of writing. These include workload and the ability to take up offers or give to particular papers the time and attention they need, while staying within the constraints of multiple deadlines. It also includes a degree of prioritising and strategizing. I am privileged to be in a position where I receive ample time and support for my research, and do not have the pressures of thinking about promotions anymore. This has changed how I approach writing, including the sense of stress that it can create. Other pressures, however, continue to frame how I think about what piece of writing to accept or not (from decisions about the REF to ensuring that I deliver on what I had promised to my research funder). Here, I have imagined the invitation as one that I would accept and would be able to approach with enough time to be 'calm and composed': the real-life version of this process is likely to feel more rushed, more stressful, and more riddled with self-doubt than its imagined version.

References

Adams, V. (2002). Randomized Controlled Crime: Postcolonial Sciences in Alternative Medicine Research. *Social Studies of Science, 32*(5/6), 659–690.

Bivins, R. (2010). *Alternative Medicine?: A History*. Oxford University Press.

Bora, A. (2008). Scientific Norms, Legal Facts, and the Politics of Knowledge. In N. Stehr & B. Weiler (Eds.), *Who Owns Knowledge? Knowledge and the Law* (pp. 67–86). Transaction.

Cloatre, E. (2019). Law and Biomedicine and the Making of "Genuine" Traditional Medicines in Global Health. *Critical Public Health, 29*(4), 424–434.

Cloatre, E., & Enright, M. (2017). "On the Perimeter of the Lawful": Enduring Illegality in the Irish Family Planning Movement, 1972–1985. *Journal of Law and Society, 44*(4), 471–500.

De Genova, N. (2013). Spectacles of Migrant "Illegality": The Scene of Exclusion, the Obscene of Inclusion. *Ethnic and Racial Studies, 36*(7), 1180–1198.

Ehrenreich, B., & English, D. (2010). *Witches, Midwives and Nurses*. The Feminist Press.

Epstein, S. (1996). *Impure Science: AIDS, Activism and the Politics of Knowledge*. University of California Press.

Ewick, P., & Silbey, S. S. (1998). *The Common Place of Law: Stories from Everyday Life*. University of Chicago Press.

Fassin, D., & Fassin, E. (1988). Traditional Medicine and the Stakes of Legitimation in Senegal. *Social Science and Medicine, 27*(4), 353–357.

Hampshire, K. R., & Asiedu Owusu, S. (2013). Grandfathers, Google, and Dreams: Medical Pluralism, Globalization, and New Healing Encounters in Ghana. *Medical Anthropology, 32*(3), 247–265.

Haraway, D. (1994). A Game of Cat's Cradle: Science Studies, Feminist Theory, Cultural Studies. *Configurations, 2*(1), 59–71.

Haraway, D. (2007). Situated Knowledges: The Science Question in Feminism and the Privilege of a Partial Perspective. In K. Asdal et al. (Eds.), *Technoscience: The Politics of Intervention* (p. 109). Unipub.

Harding, S. G. (1991). *Whose Science? Whose Knowledge? Thinking from Women's Lives*. Cornell University Press.

Harding, S. G. (1998). *Is Science Multicultural?: Postcolonialisms, Feminisms, and Epistemologies*. Indiana University Press.

Jasanoff, S. (2006). Ordering Knowledge, Ordering Society. In S. Jasanoff (Ed.), *States of Knowledge: The Co-Production of Science and Social Order*. Routledge.

Langwick, S. (2006). Geographies of Medicine: Interrogating the Boundary Between "Traditional" and "Modern" Medicine in Colonial Tanganyika. In T. J. Luedke & H. G. West (Eds.), *Borders and Healers: Broking Therapeutic Resources in Southeast Africa* (pp. 143–165). Indiana University Press.

Langwick, S. (2011). *Bodies, Politics, and African Healing*. Indiana University Press.

Latour, B., & Porter, C. (1993). *We Have Never Been Modern*. Harvard University Press.

Law, J., & Mol, A. (1995). Notes on Materiality and Sociality. *The Sociological Review, 43*, 274–294.

Mezey, N. (2001). Out of the Ordinary: Law, Power, Culture, and the Commonplace. *Law and Social Inquiry, 26*, 145–167.

Mol, A. (2003). *The Body Multiple*. Duke University Press.

Osseo-Asare, A. (2014). *Bitter Roots: The Search for Healing Plants in Africa*. University of Chicago Press.

Pordié, L., & Gaudillère, J.-P. (2013). Industrialiser les médicaments ayurvédiques: les voies indiennes de l'innovation pharmaceutique. *Autrepart, 63*(4), 123–143.

Ramsey, M. (1999). Alternative Medicine in Modern France. *Medical History, 43*(3), 286–322.

Roitman, J., Comaroff, J., & Comaroff, J. (2006). The Ethics of Illegality in the Chad Basin. In J. Comaroff & J. L. Comaroff (Eds.), *Law and Disorder in the Postcolony*. University of Chicago Press.

Silbey, S. S. (2005). After Legal Consciousness. *Annual Review of Law and Social Science, 1*, 323–368.

Urquiza Haas, N., & Cloatre, E. (2021). The Challenge of "Evidence": Research and Regulation of Traditional and Non-Conventional Medicines. In G. Laurie et al. (Eds.), *Cambridge Handbook of Health Research Regulation*. Cambridge University Press.

Vasconi, E. (2016). Witchcraft, Medicine and British Colonial Rule: Anthropological Analysis of Colonial Documents in the Gold Coast. In M. Pavanello (Ed.), *Perspectives on African Witchcraft*. Routledge.

Vaughan, M. (1991). *Curing Their Ills: Colonial Power and African Illness*. Stanford University Press.

Wahlberg, A. (2006). Bio-politics and the Promotion of Traditional Herbal Medicine in Vietnam. *Health, 10*(2), 123–147.

Wahlberg, A. (2007). A Quackery with a Difference – New Medical Pluralism and the Problem of "Dangerous Practitioners" in the United Kingdom. *Social Science and Medicine, 65*(11), 2307–2016.

CHAPTER 4

Researching Racialised Bodies in Higher Education: From Statistics to Storytelling

Suhraiya Jivraj

Abstract Quantitative data, particularly in the form of statistics measuring student attainment along racial/ethnic lines, has been the predominant evidence base for law and policymaking in relation to higher education institutions tackling racial inequalities in the sector. In challenging the rendering of racialised bodies in the academy into 'stats', I instead explore a qualitative approach foregrounding racialised experiences, their complexities, nuances and intersections, often left absent or flattened when using quantitative methodologies. I draw on counter-storytelling as a form of experiential and embodied knowledge production as developed through critical race theory relating to education, as well as in decolonial studies' approaches to research. Working with counter-storytelling—as a method for researching the experiences of racialised student *and* staff bodies—builds on a tradition of transmitting knowledge that has already established creative ways to *ethically* co-produce, analyse, and understand socio-economic—including educational—inequalities. This creative and ethical approach takes us beyond the academic strictures and limitations—including form—of the 'European/Western canon' whilst also exposing its power in knowledge production. Understanding and working within this frame can loosen the powerful grip of this canon and its modern quantitative forms, by making space for racialised bodies to be able to 'speak' about themselves.

S. Jivraj (✉)
University of Kent, Canterbury, UK
e-mail: s.jivraj@kent.ac.uk

D. Herman, C. Parsley (eds.), *Interdisciplinarities*, Palgrave Socio-Legal Studies, https://doi.org/10.1007/978-3-030-89297-5_4

Keywords Qualitative methods • Counter-storytelling • Decolonial studies • Embodied knowledge • Racialised bodies • Higher education

Introduction: Methodological Choices

> I look at them as they sit some shy unable to speak for fear they might choke
> tentative and then wide eyed/brash/nervous/swallowing hard, biting
> down harder.
> then she flings her words across the room so fast she can't be interrupted, teeth
> flailing. I want to ask, what skin did you shed just then?
> Share a piece of what made you untouchable. (Olufemi, 2019, p. 112)

Since 2015, the UK and elsewhere has seen a resurgence of protest against racism in our universities, from the curricula and lack of diverse reading lists to lack of safe space within classrooms and on campuses (Jivraj, 2020a). These concerns have become further amplified by the Black Lives Matter and related movements which highlight the precarity of the lives and bodies of racialised people, especially the Black diaspora in the Global North. The accumulative physical, mental, emotional and other effects of these experiences on students, many of whom may also be experiencing historical trauma passed through generations, including from slavery, exile and other forms of violence, reverberate through Lola Olufemi's words above from her poem titled 'Space' (2019). Like her co-contributors to *A Fly Girl's Guide to University: Being a Woman of Colour at Cambridge and Other Institutions of Power and Elitism*, and so many other students of colour[1] speaking and acting out, Olufemi powerfully recounts the visceral impact of being a racialised student body in the academy.

Yet, this body of work—authored by and foregrounding the experiences of both students and staff or faculty of colour—often remains at the margins of debate; and therefore, crucially, has also remained excluded from law and policymaking that seeks to address racial inequalities and discrimination within higher education institutions (HEIs). Rather, HEIs have been required to implement policies to tackle racial inequalities based on a quantitative research approach. Official statistics from AdvanceHE (2019) recorded a national 'BME degree attainment gap' of 13.2 per cent. This means that 80.9 per cent of white students received what is considered a good degree (first or 2:1) compared with 67.7 per cent of BME students (ibid.). Even within these

[1] As I have outlined elsewhere (Jivraj, 2020c), my own preferred term is 'racialised people' or 'people of colour' (POC) as opposed to BME (Black Minority Ethnic) or BAME (Black, Asian, Minority Ethnic) as it avoids the language of 'minoritising' which can contribute to racialised thinking. 'POC' is also a term that emanates from women of colour activism and solidarity politics rather than arising from policy discourse. Whilst it has been critiqued for being a prominently US term, it is now more widely used globally, but of course every term comes from its own specific genealogy and historical and socio-political context and therefore cannot be fully representative. On critiques of the use of BME/BAME see further: Adebisi (2019b), Joseph (2020), D'Clark (2018), Andrews (2020).

collectivised narratives about 'BME student attainment', there is a hierarchy created through a sub-categorising within the groups, justified by statistics that seemingly demonstrate a much narrower attainment gap for Chinese (4.3 per cent), mixed (3.7 per cent) and Asian Indian 'qualifiers' (aka students) (5.2 per cent) (ibid.). The gap, according to the statistics, is 'particularly pronounced' for students from 'other' Black (24.6 per cent), Black African (23.9 per cent) and Black Caribbean (21.7 per cent) backgrounds (AdvanceHE, 2019).

There are many problems associated with and developing policies relying on statistics from these kinds of quantitative data collection methods. Even the Office for Students (OfS), the UK universities regulator that legally[2] requires universities to address attainment gaps, acknowledges that the statistics do not reveal how 'within every ethnic group there is a subgroup of individuals who are more disadvantaged or underrepresented in higher education than others in the group' (OfS, 2018). However, interrogating the statistics for the invisibility of subgroups and intersections of disability, race, religion and gender in these reports is not enough. As many scholars of colour have now highlighted, the rhetoric on lack of achievement by students of colour perpetuates what is referred to as a 'deficit model'—or in the words of Robbie Shilliam—the belief that 'black students arrive at the gates of university with pronounced social and cultural deficits garnered from their familial and community upbringing' (2015, p. 59). There is of course a perverse irony here that policies seeking to raise attainment are doing so in ways that reinforce racial categorising reminiscent of colonial policies based on hierarchy of the races and racial intelligence (Saini, 2019) that replicate the idea of a biological racial 'essence' (Ahmed, 2002).

Thus, in reflecting on the constellation of bodies for a research project on racial inequalities in higher education, including student, staff, the university and even bodies of knowledge, the methodological choices we make can have a profound importance in terms of both social justice outcomes *and* doing research ethically. The methods we choose can either expose or keep hidden power in the process of knowledge (co-)production, and how and where that knowledge comes to be used. For example, if we want our research to be grounded in and positively impact the lives of research participants/those being researched then we need to be mindful that our methodological choices lead to sufficiently nuanced research rather than perpetuating and/or reinforcing harms such as racialisation. I would therefore want to explore alternative methodological choices to the quantitative data collection resulting in statistics measuring 'attainment gaps' which remains the current dominant model for

[2] Pursuant to the Higher Education and Research Act (HERA) 2017, universities are now required to address awarding disparities (more commonly known as 'attainment gaps'). The OfS, also established by HERA (section 1), is tasked with a number of functions (section 2(1)) in relation to the English higher education sector, including registering universities (section 3) with regard to conditions such as promoting 'equality of opportunity in connection with access to and participation' (section 2(e)). The OfS has published targets to eliminate inequalities as well as guidance for universities who must have access and participation plans working towards achieving the national (OfS) targets (Jivraj, 2020c).

universities to tackle racial inequalities. Instead, I would take a qualitative methods approach, which foregrounds capturing the complexities of lived and intersecting realities to produce experiential knowledge, for example, through forms of storytelling. This is an approach used in both critical race theory (CRT), including in relation to education, and in decolonial studies. The latter highlights the importance of the ethics of the researcher in relation to how they conduct their research and engage with their participants. Both fields of study reveal how counter-narratives to the dominant modes of theory and praxis could therefore lead to other avenues of addressing intersecting racial inequalities in higher education.

Racialised Bodies in HEIs: Counter-storytelling

To research experiences of racialised bodies in HEIs, I would begin with a literature search on (anti)racism and the university and soon come up with seminal works from British CRT including *Building the Anti-Racist University* by Professor Shirley Anne Tate and Paul Bagguley (2017). CRT is itself a *body of knowledge* which emerged from the work of scholars of colour—predominantly lawyers in the United States—who were engaging in a political and legal struggle against racism from the 1970s.[3] CRT developed in the UK, particularly coalescing with critical legal studies (CLS) in the work of, for example, the late Professor Peter Fitzpatrick (1992, 2001),[4] as well as in the field of education studies (e.g. Ladson-Billings & Tate, 1995; Gillborn, 2005; Pilkington, 2013; Alexander & Arday, 2015; Arday & Mirza, 2018; Gillborn et al., 2018). There is also, notably, a branch of CRT which explores issues of race and racism through the lens of Black British Feminism (Mirza, 1997, 2018) which is resurging once again (Emejulu & Sobande, 2019).

CRT is not a homogeneous body of scholarship, and, as I have explored elsewhere (Jivraj, 2020a), it has a range of perspectives on whether an anti-racist or 'decolonised' university is even possible. Nevertheless, what is important for this research trajectory is to appreciate the convergent perspectives on how we can understand, conceptualise and analyse the universities, particularly in (former) colonial metropoles, as being embedded in and having benefitted from a *legacy* of systemic racism (Bhambra et al., 2018). We would therefore want to examine how universities continue to perpetuate systemic racism and racialisation in particular, including through their 'equalities' strategies (Ahmed, 2007, 2012; Tate & Page, 2018). As Ahmed reminds us, 'the term "racialized bodies" invites us to think of the multiple processes whereby bodies come to be seen as 'having' a racial identity' (2002, p. 46). This identity is not

[3] Derrick Bell (1987, 1995), Richard Delgado (see Matsuda et al., 1993; Delgado & Stefancic, 2001), Charles Lawrence (Matsuda et al., 1993), Mari Matsuda (Matsuda et al., 1993; Matsuda, 1996), Patricia Williams (1991) and Kimberlé Crenshaw (1989; see also 1993) are some of the prominent CRT scholars.

[4] See also the Critical Legal Thinking blog: https://criticallegalthinking.com/ accessed 26 August 2021.

predetermined by skin colour or other phenotypical features or characteristics but rather what 'takes place in time and space' that produces 'race' itself (ibid.). It is therefore the processes of racialisation—articulated through counter-storytelling—that we want to pay attention to; particularly as the same depth of detail and nuance cannot be captured by qualitative statistical data.

Instead, what we need is to recognise these racialisation processes and their impact on the educational experiences of students by listening and meaningfully hearing what 'takes place' for them, during and within the time and space they are in HEIs. When we begin to better understand by actively listening to what produces 'race' for students—and also staff—of colour and how it is manifested through the different senses, or what Olufemi describes as needing to 'shed skin' when those bodies feel they are 'choking', then, and only then, can we begin the work tackling inequalities, including through law and policy formation. Active hearing enables responses to be made more effectively (Jivraj, 2020b), and that is why for me the 'gap' is not with students of colour as a 'body of students'—currently captured as 'attainment gap' statistics—but rather a *failure* by HEIs as an academic body to listen and meaningfully *hear* students when they speak or recount their experiences of racism in the curriculum, classroom and campus. So, we turn to the qualitative method of 'counter-storytelling', but before we explore the work from and about the recent student movements to 'decolonise' or 'liberate' their universities, curriculum and so on,[5] we would want to first explore the genealogy of the method, where it comes from (context) and what it seeks to achieve that may be different to other (qualitative) approaches and methods.

This method was developed within CRT as a means of knowledge production around social inequalities in the lives of Black people and other people of colour in the United States and beyond. It is therefore a more meaningful premise for law and policymaking aimed at tackling educational inequalities that seek to avoid the reductive rendering of bodies into a set of statistics rather than as complex people with the focus being on experiences of racialisation, or how race comes into being within HEIs (Solórzano & Yosso, 2002a, b; see also Doharty et al., 2021). As Gloria Ladson Billings (2013) explains, counter-storytelling brings to our attention broader issues of social justice, including beyond individual racial struggles.

One of the earliest and most well-known examples of this method is the work of Derrick Bell. In his book *And We Are Not Saved: The Elusive Quest for Racial Justice* (1987),[6] Bell discusses civil rights issues through ten 'chronicles' divided into three parts. He takes the reader through a journey on 'The Real Hurdles to Racial Justice' in part one, 'The Social Affliction of Racism' in part

[5] See, for example, Black (2014), NUS (2016), SOAS (2017), Keele Student Union et al. (2018), RMFO (2018), DecoloniseUoK et al. (2020), NUS (2021).

[6] Which develops an earlier version of his work as a foreword entitled 'The Civil Rights Chronicles' in the *Harvard Law Review* (Bell, 1985) marking the bicentenary of the US Constitution.

two and 'Divining a Nation's Salvation' (part three), which ends with his 'ultimate civil rights strategy' told through the chronicle of 'The Black crime cure' (pp. 245–248). Each chronicle features a narrator and *alter ego* 'Geneva Crenshaw' who, as we are told in the 'The Chronicle of the DeVine Gift' (pp. 140–161), feels overburdened with work as the only African American law professor in a prestigious law school. By using the device of allegory, Bell is able to share his analysis of his own situation—and others he knows—as a professor at an elite US university, in this case also Harvard Law School. In this chronicle, Bell goes on to imagine what life might be like for Geneva if this high-profile predominately white law school would reach a 'tipping point' if 'too many' candidates of colour were to be hired. The writing allows Bell to draw from his experience to analyse wider issues such as affirmative action seeking to remedy aspects of racism in the workplace, including hiring practices.

However, as Ladson-Billings notes, this then 'quickly branches off into a speculative tale allowing for different possibilities' including how such 'equalities' measures can reach their limits ('tipping point') and even backfire (2013, p. 43). The tension between working towards constitutional guarantees for equality for all and the realities of everyday lived experiences of racialisation is powerfully rendered through these chronicles right to the end in Bell's final story. Two decades on from writing this story, we can look back at Bell's work and reflect on the possibilities that he imagined in the current context, particularly given the significant proliferation of literature and research from different disciplinary fields now available on the experiences of people of colour in the academy (Gabriel & Tate, 2017; Rollock, 2019; Bhopal & Pitkin, 2020). One significant theme that runs through this body of literature is that racialisation still impacts workload, and so much more for people of colour, particularly (Black) women, who have to overcome significant structural hurdles to even make it through the 'gates' beyond undergraduate level (Miller, 2016; Rollock, 2019).[7] The power of counter-storytelling is not just about effecting 'change' in the sense of legal reform or new policies, when this can so often be 'non-performative' in the sense of doing little meaningful structural anti-racist work whilst still *performing* doing the work (Ahmed, 2007; Bhopal & Pitkin, 2020). Rather, it is about being able to reflect on these conditions and how the processes of racialisation are working and impacting on racialised bodies in our own voices and methods of articulation—'shedding of skin'—and not only just making them known for an external reader.[8]

The CRT method of counter-storytelling also goes beyond education in its exploration and research of racial injustice and how it manifests materially in

[7] There is also now more scholarly work on experiences of racialised staff in the academy, for example on issues of gendered ethnic pay and promotion gaps (Rollock, 2016; Arday & Mirza, 2018; Bhopal, 2018; Rollock, 2019) as well as labour conditions more generally (UCLTV, 2014; Morgan, 2016; Gabriel & Tate, 2017; Doharty et al., 2021).

[8] See, for example, Rollock (2019) and the accompanying exhibition of portraits of the professors interviewed by Rollock and displayed by the South Bank Centre in 2020: see https://www.southbankcentre.co.uk/whats-on/art-exhibitions/phenomenal-women accessed 28 June 2021.

people's lives. In the work of another US-based law professor, Patricia Williams, in her seminal text *The Alchemy of Race and Rights*, she states that she uses 'all sorts of literary devices, including parable, parody and poetry' (1991, p. 8) to explore property law.[9] In her chapter entitled 'Gilded Lilies and Liberal Guilt', she discusses doctrines of contract and value woven into how it felt to find her enslaved great-great grandmothers' contract of sale. Similarly, she explores material conditions relating again to housing and poverty to the contemporary story of the ease with which her male white colleague can find accommodation compared to her own experience when arriving for a new job at Harvard university. When I first read this account—as a younger aspiring legal academic—it resonated for me and contextualised my experiences of racialisation impacting my housing search as a junior scholar of colour. For Williams—and so many racialised scholars—there is a *power* that comes through in understanding law, policy and societal norms embedded in racialised and colonial thinking and the embodied impact it can have:

> As I said, this is the sort of morning when I hate being a lawyer, a teacher, and just about everything else in my life. It's all I can do to feed the cats. I let my hair stream wildly and the eyes rollback in my head. So you should know that this is one of those mornings when I refuse to compose myself properly; you should know you are dealing with someone who is writing this in an old terry bath robe with a little fringe of blue and white tassels dangling from the hem, trying to decide if she is stupid or crazy. (1991, p. 4)

The power lies in the *acknowledgment* of the visceral consequences of racialisation for her as a faculty member who is a woman of colour (see also, on the 'Politics of Exhaustion', Mirza, 2017; Emejulu & Bassel, 2020). William's statement is powerful in its refusal to hide the embodied impact of racialisation and refusal to perform the 'resilience' that so many universities are training their staff to develop (Gill & Orgad, 2018; McRobbie, 2020). As decolonial studies scholars Walter Mignolo and Rolando Vazquez state (2013), it is crucial to find ways to heal from 'colonial wounds', not just through resistance but also 're-existence' or showing up with *all* parts of our embodied selves.

Listening to and Empowering Students: Decolonial Research Ethics

> I am not your data, nor am I your vote bank,
> I am not your project, or any exotic museum project,
> I am not the soul waiting to be harvested,
> Nor am I the lab where your theories are tested. (Xaxa, 2011)

[9] See also Rose (1990).

Counter-storytelling as a method of exploring racial injustices in society and education is now part of a transhistorical lineage of what Lama Rod Owens (2020) refers to as 'wisdom texts'. These CRT and decolonial studies texts are drawn upon by scholars, students and activists of colour to explore the impact of racialisation on bodies of colour. As we have seen from the stories explored above, bodies here can include the physical, mental, emotional, spiritual and subtle energy (nervous system), as well as collective body (Owens, 2020). If we turn to researching the specific experiences of students of colour foregrounding experiential knowledge as articulated through storytelling and other creative forms, what will we find and what will we learn that we cannot discover from using a quantitative method?

We know from students themselves that racial inequalities in HEIs need to be tackled. The 'data' is available, ranging from research by collective bodies such as the National Union of Students (NUS), or from various student movements including 'elite' universities, such as Oxford and the Rhodes Must Fall Movement, Oxford (RMFO) (2018), to post-1960s 'red brick' universities like Kent (DecoloniseUKC, 2019) or Keele (Keele Student Union et al., 2018) producing manifestos and recommendations to tackle racism on campus, as well as a lack of diversity within the curriculum and staff body (see also UCLTV, 2014). This 'data' demonstrates how the different forms of racialisation experienced can have a significant impact on mental and physical well-being and therefore also eventual degree marks. However, we also know that these students' experiences are often absent, invisibilised or 'utilised' at policy levels to fit within the institutional Equalities, Diversity and Inclusion or student success frameworks (Memon & Jivraj, 2020). This 'co-optation' can result in a lack of meaningful change, perpetuation of the sense that students are 'space invaders' (as Joseph-Salisbury, 2019 puts it),[10] and therefore result in continued demands for change.

In examining this work and the student stories, we realise that the form of this research ranges from academic texts (Sian, 2019) to poetry and the spoken word (Manzoor-Khan, 2019),[11] and (feminist) zines (Building the Antiracist Classroom Collective, 2020), as well as digital outputs such as podcasts (Memon & Olugboyega, 2020) or artwork including photography (Ahmet, 2020; Afro-Diasporic Legal Network, 2021). What we can learn from this body of work is how the processes of racialisation in HEIs come about, their impacts on bodies of colour, and the specific demands students are making from their universities to tackle racial inequalities need to be articulated in different ways. I will return to this point below.

There is, therefore, already a significant field of literature and other material that gives the researcher data to work with. Whilst some of this work speaks to

[10] Drawing on the work of Puwar (2004).

[11] See, for example, https://research.kent.ac.uk/sergj/embodied-writing-workshop-reflections/ and https://research.kent.ac.uk/sergj/decolonise-uok-stories-of-unbelonging-with-lowkey/ both accessed 28 June 2021.

broader and more well-known issues of 'decolonising' the curriculum and reading lists, there is also now a rich data set in the context of specific universities and their student experience (see, e.g. Akel, 2019).[12] We could focus on any number of the myriad of issues that have been identified, including, for example, how students experience the architecture of campuses or university sites, including statues associated with racist practices, policies and views, from Rhodes at Oxford (RMFO, 2018) to the academic and inventor of the term 'eugenics' Francis Galton at University College London (UCLTV, 2014), the slave trader Edward Colstan in Bristol (Adebisi, 2019a) or economist John Maynard Keynes and philosopher John Locke at Kent (Misra, 2020a, b). We know from the quantitative data that the built environment has an embodied impact on students and particularly those racialised as non-white.

Students from movements such as Decolonise Keele or Kent have produced manifestos with demands for the specific changes they want to see. One key demand at Kent, for example, has been in relation to well-being and mental health services, seeking regular and specific sessions for students of colour, including with specific disabilities (DecoloniseUKC, 2019, p. 25). Students have repeatedly asked for counsellors/therapists of colour with an embodied understanding of transhistorical trauma compounded by everyday manifestations of racialisation (Shoko, 2020). This very specific demand would not be able to be captured or communicated through the quantitative data of attainment gaps. Moreover, the demands, which resulted from data collected by the DecoloniseUoK student researchers, trained by staff of colour, led to changes in well-being policy (Jivraj, 2020b) and subsequent appropriate staffing for services aimed at students of colour.

This process shows that counter-stories can lead to a meaningful change in tackling racial barriers within well-being services. However, the method is also powerful because of the way the data was collected, namely by and for the student stakeholders, on their own terms and where they engaged in a long-term process that was designed to be self-empowering (Jivraj, 2020b). The focus groups took place as 'decolonial cafes', in locations that the participants collectively chose—where they as racialised bodies felt safe(r)—and which took place after or as part of other capacity-building activities such as reading groups, masterclasses and creative workshops (DecoloniseUKC, 2019, p. 20). This journey of empowerment to and through storytelling also built community for those students with each other across disciplines, as well as with other Decolonise movements from Keele, Queen Mary University of London, Kings College London, Lancaster and Goldsmiths universities. The coming together of all these students from different institutions, taking up the space of a theatre stage to narrate their stories in public, as a collective body, was a powerful moment. Sitting alongside a high-profile educator and rap artist Lowkey, known for his work on getting out the Black youth vote and campaigning for justice for survivors of the fire at the London Grenfell Tower, inspired the

[12] See also Afro-Diasporic Legal Network (2020).

collective student body to be able to recognise, release and share their embodied experiences in ways that would not normally feel safe or understood in a classroom or research environment. It was a decolonial moment of not just resistance but also 're-existence' (Mignolo & Walsh, 2018).[13] In that moment, the students and their experiences were not able to be flattened by being reduced into numbers and performance targets required by the neo-liberal university, nor were they subject to exploitative framings of their experiences (Memon & Jivraj, 2020). Rather, the students themselves were centred in a powerful moment of being able to speak their truth, 'shed skin' in a space they had co-created and through creative forms (spoken word, art and music) that they had co-curated. These moments of continuing the anti-racist struggle—surviving embodied inequities whether from police/campus security brutality or hyper-surveillance, health inequalities and so on—are not just a form of resistance, but also a process whereby the visceral consequences of racialisation can be metabolised, producing a sense of (momentary) re-existence.

Doing this work and creating these moments is easier when someone, or a body of people, has done it before. When other students and scholars of colour have already left a legacy that can be followed by those to come. As such the DecoloniseUoK, RMFO and the continued building of other student movements (National Union of Students, 2021) are the latest paving stones placed on the pathway of a continuing lineage that sustains racialised bodies in the academy (Memon & Jivraj, 2020). As Richard Delgado reminds us:

> Reality, like our hopes for it, is not fixed. We construct it through conversations, through our lives together. The sad fact of race is that too few of these conversations ever take place; to that extent our lives are diminished. Books like *And We Are Not Saved* help us avoid this impoverishment and may, perhaps, set us on a more positive course in dealing with our most intractable problem. (1988, p. 947)

Drawing from this lineage of scholarship is therefore essential to spiritual, mental and emotional and therefore physical survival of racialised bodies in HEIs. At this point, it is important to explore why 'survival' is so important and how that leads us to drawing from and building a decolonial ethics of research, in relation to tackling racial inequalities in higher education. In their seminal text 'Refusing Research', Eve Tuck and K. Wayne Yang remind us that:

> The ethical standards of the academic industrial complex are a recent development, and like so many post-civil rights reforms, do not always do enough to ensure that social science research is deeply ethical, meaningful, or useful for the individual or community being researched. Social science often works to collect stories of pain and humiliation in the lives of those being researched for commodification. (2014, p. 223)

[13] https://research.kent.ac.uk/sergj/decolonise-uok-stories-of-unbelonging-with-lowkey/ accessed 28 June 2021.

Instead, they ask us to reflect on how we can 'learn' and 'respect' what we hear in the stories, whilst also refusing a historically embedded 'gaze' of researchers upon racialised bodies (ibid.). As decolonial and other scholars have demonstrated, this gaze is a legacy from various periods of history, including settler colonialism (Tuck & Yang, 2012; Tuhiwai Smith, 2012; Tuhiwai Smith et al., 2019). It is therefore crucial to avoid reinforcing this gaze by being honest and open about power relations and how research and researchers can be complicit in upholding those relations. One way to do this is to draw on research where participants have led in the research process and/or co-produced the work, rather than being the mere 'objects' or the 'qualifiers' of the study, as we saw above in the AdvanceHE statistical data. As Tuck and Yang and many other theorists who draw on storytelling as method state, 'refusal' within research humanises researchers (2014, p. 223). It also empowers research participants to wrestle with the extraneous difficulties of being embodied, namely being present in those bodies that are subject to the various continued traumas of racialisation, which reinforces disassociation resulting from wanting to escape from that (past and present) pain (Mignolo & Vazquez, 2013; Owens, 2020). In drawing upon counter-storytelling and contributing to its legacy as a method, we participate in exposing and addressing the embodied impact upon the emotional, spiritual, mental and physical parts of racialised bodies through empowerment to self-articulate (Mignolo, 2009; Zahara, 2016).

Concluding Remarks: Towards Transformative Research

Researching racialised bodies in the academy has brought into the frame the many other bodies in connection and contention around them: the university body, its faculty bodies, bodies of knowledge that make up the curriculum and even the bodies of famous DWMs (dead white men) who become enshrined in the built environment of campuses through names of buildings or other forms of memorialisation. In reflecting on this constellation of bodies as the object of my enquiry, my methodological choice has been to explore counter-storytelling as a form of knowledge production using qualitative methods. This is a different approach to the more prevalent route of quantitative data collection measuring attainment gaps as a way of tackling racial inequalities in higher education which is unable to capture the complexities of lived experiences to produce experiential knowledge, a key aspect of a CRT method. This is not to say that there is no place at all for quantitative methods (Bhopal & Pitkin, 2020). As I explore elsewhere, when the two are combined with the commitment to effect meaningful change, processes around well-being, for example, can be notably improved (Jivraj, 2020b).

However, the real transformative potential of working with counter-storytelling—as a method for researching the experiences of racialised student *and* staff bodies—is important for three interlinked reasons. Firstly, there is a socio-political impetus for using counter-storytelling itself, building on a tradition of transmitting knowledge including history through oral and other (artistic) forms. Secondly, this *lineage*—continued through CRT, decolonial studies and counter-storytelling in particular—has already established creative ways to *ethically* collate, analyse and understand socio-economic—including educational—inequalities. This creative and ethical approach takes us beyond the academic strictures and limitations—including form—of the 'European/western canon'. Thirdly, centring experiences of inequalities in HEIs that have been largely marginalised through storytelling also exposes power in knowledge production of a canon built on colonial violence. Understanding and working within this frame can loosen the powerful grip of this canon and its modern quantitative forms, by making space for racialised bodies to be able to 'speak' about themselves, including in complex intersectional ways.

References

Adebisi, F. (2019a, October 28). Decolonising the University of Bristol. *African Skies*. Retrieved June 28, 2021, from https://folukeafrica.com/decolonising-the-university-of-bristol/

Adebisi, F. (2019b, July 8). The Only Accurate Part of "BAME" is the "and"... *African Skies*. https://folukeafrica.com/the-only-acceptable-part-of-bame-is-the-and

AdvanceHE. (2019). *Equality in Higher Education: Students Statistical Report 2019*. Retrieved June 28, 2021, from https://www.advance-he.ac.uk/knowledge-hub/equality-higher-education-statistical-report-2019

Afro-Diasporic Legal Network. (2020). *Eight BME Societies Statement of Solidarity and Call to Action to the University of Kent*. Retrieved June 28, 2021, from https://medium.com/@afrodiasporiclegalnetwork/bme-societies-submit-a-statement-of-solidarity-demands-to-the-university-of-kent-a353c351e9df

Afro-Diasporic Legal Network. (2021). *Photo Campaign: Black Student Experiences*. Retrieved June 28, 2021, from https://issuu.com/blackliberationcollectivekent/docs/adln_photo_campaign2021

Ahmed, S. (2002). Racialized Bodies. In M. Evans & E. Lee (Eds.), *Real Bodies*. Palgrave.

Ahmed, S. (2007). You End Up Doing the Document Rather Than the Doing: Diversity, Race Equality and the Politics of Documentations. *Ethnic and Racial Studies, 30*(4), 590–609.

Ahmed, S. (2012). *On Being Included: Racism and Diversity in Institutional Life*. Duke University Press.

Ahmet, A. (2020). Who Is Worthy of a Place on These Walls? Postgraduate Students, UK Universities, and Institutional Racism. *Area, 52*(4), 678–686.

Akel, S. (2019). *Insider-outsider: The Role of Race in Shaping the Experiences of Black and Minority Ethnic Students*. Retrieved June 28, 2021, from https://www.gold.ac.uk/media/docs/reports/Insider-Outsider-Report-191008.pdf

Alexander, C., & Arday, J. (2015). *Aiming Higher Race, Inequality and Diversity in the Academy*. Runnymede Trust. Retrieved June 28, 2021, from https://www.runnymedetrust.org/uploads/Aiming%20Higher.pdf

Andrews, K. (2020, November 13). I Am not your BAME Person. *Make It Plain*. Retrieved June 28, 2021, from https://make-it-plain.org/2020/11/13/i-am-not-your-bame-person/

Arday, J., & Mirza, H. (Eds.). (2018). *Dismantling Race in Higher Education: Racism, Whiteness and Decolonising the Academy*. Palgrave Macmillan.

Bell, D. A. (1985). The Supreme Court, 1984 Term-foreword: The Civil Rights Chronicles. *Harvard Law Review, 99*, 4–83.

Bell, D. A. (1987). *And We Are Not Saved: The Elusive Quest for Racial Justice*. Books Inc.

Bell, D. A. (1995). Who's Afraid of Critical Race Theory? *University of Illinois Law Review, 4*, 893–910.

Bhambra, G. K., Gebrial, D., & Nisanc ṃıoğlu, N. (2018). Introduction: Decolonizing the University? In G. K. Bhambra, D. Gebrial, & N. Nisanc ṃıoğlu (Eds.), *Decolonizing the University* (pp. 2–10). Pluto Press.

Bhopal, K. (2018). *White Privilege: The Myth of a Post-racial Society*. Bristol University Press.

Bhopal, K., & Pitkin, C. (2020). Same Old Story, Just a Different Policy: Race and Policy Making in Higher Education in the UK. *Race Ethnicity and Education, 23*(4), 530–547.

Black, L. N. (2014, December 8). Why Isn't my Professor Black? On Reflection. *DTMH*. Retrieved June 28, 2021, from http://www.dtmh.ucl.ac.uk/isnt-professor-black-reflection/

Building the Antiracist Classroom Collective. (2020). Zine-making for Anti-racist Learning and Action. In DecoloniseUoK Collective, D. Thomas, & S. Jivraj (Eds.), *Towards Decolonising the University: A Kaleidoscope for Empowered Action* (pp. 51–58). Counterpress.

Crenshaw, K. (1989). Demarginalizing the Intersection of Race and Sex: A Black Feminist Critique of Antidiscrimination Doctrine, Feminist Theory and Antiracist Politics. *University of Chicago Law School, 1*, 139–168.

Crenshaw, K. (1993). Mapping the Margins: Intersectionality, Identity Politics, and Violence Against Women of Color. *Stanford Law Review, 43*(6), 1241–1299.

D'Clark, R. S. (2018, August 11). B.A.M.E. Is Lame. *Shades of Noir*. Retrieved June 28, 2021, from https://shadesofnoir.org.uk/b-a-m-e-is-l-a-m-e/

DecoloniseUKC. Manifesto 2019. Republished in DecoloniseUoK Collective, (2020). D. Thomas, & S. Jivraj (Eds.), *Towards Decolonising the University: A Kaleidoscope for Empowered Action*. (pp 17-30). Counterpress.

Delgado, R. (1988). Derrick Bell and the Ideology of Racial Reform: Will We Ever Be Saved? A Review Essay. *Yale Law Journal, 97*(5), 923–947.

Delgado, R., & Stefancic, J. (2001). *Critical Race Theory: An Introduction*. New York University Press.

Doharty, N., Madriaga, M., & Joseph-Salisbury, R. (2021). The University Went to "Decolonise" and All They Brought Back Was Lousy Diversity Double-Speak! Critical Race Counter-Stories from Faculty of Colour in "Decolonial" Times. *Educational Philosophy and Theory, 53*(3), 233–244.

Emejulu, A., & Bassel, L. (2020). The Politics of Exhaustion. *City, 24*(1–2), 400–406.

Emejulu, A., & Sobande, F. (2019). *To Exist Is to Resist: Black Feminism in Europe*. Pluto Press.

Fitzpatrick, P. (1992). *The Mythology of Modern Law*. Routledge.

Fitzpatrick, P. (2001). *Modernism and the Grounds of Law*. Cambridge University Press.

Gabriel, D., & Tate, S. A. (2017). *Inside the Ivory Tower: Narratives of Women of Colour Surviving and Thriving in British Academia*. Trentham Books.

Gill, R., & Orgad, S. (2018). The Amazing Bounce-backable Woman: Resilience and the Psychological Turn in Neoliberalism. *Sociological Research Online, 23*(2), 477–495.

Gillborn, D. (2005). Education Policy as an Act of White Supremacy: Whiteness, Critical Race Theory and Education Reform. *Journal of Education Policy, 20*(4), 485–505.

Gillborn, D., Dixson, A., Ladson Billings, G., Parker, L., Rollock, N., & Warmington, P. (Eds.). (2018). *Critical Race Theory in Education.* Routledge.

Jivraj, S. (2020a). Decolonizing the Academy—Between a Rock and a Hard Place. *Interventions, 22*(4), 552–573.

Jivraj, S. (2020b). Decolonising the University: Success, Pitfalls and Next Steps. In DecoloniseUoK Collective, D. Thomas, & S. Jivraj (Eds.), *Towards Decolonising the University: A Kaleidoscope for Empowered Action* (pp. 167–180). Counterpress.

Jivraj, S. (2020c). *Towards an Anti-Racist Legal Pedagogy: A Resource.* Retrieved June 28, 2021, from https://research.kent.ac.uk/decolonising-law-schools/

Joseph, C. (2020, June 25). Bookmark This: The BAME Acronym Is Often Reductive and Lazy. *gal-dem.* Retrieved June 28, 2021, from https://gal-dem.com/bookmark-this-are-acronyms-like-bame-a-nonsense/

Joseph-Salisbury, R. (2019). Institutionalised Whiteness, Racial Microaggressions and Black Bodies Out of Place in Higher Education. *Whiteness and Education, 4*(1), 1–17.

Keele Student Union, Keele Postgraduate Association and Keele University College Union. (2018). *Manifesto for Decolonising the Curriculum.* Retrieved June 28, 2021, from https://www.keele.ac.uk/equalitydiversity/equalityframeworksandactivities/equalityawardsandreports/equalityawards/raceequalitycharter/keeledecolonisingthecurriculumnetwork/#keele-manifesto-for-decolonising-the-curriculum

Ladson-Billings, G. (2013). Critical Race Theory—What It Is Not! In M. Lynn & D. Dixson (Eds.), *Handbook of Critical Race Theory in Education* (pp. 34–47). Routledge.

Ladson-Billings, G., & Tate, W. (1995). Toward a Critical Race Theory of Education. *Teachers College Record, 97*(1), 47–68.

Manzoor-Khan, S. (2019). *Postcolonial Banter.* Verve Poetry Press.

Matsuda, M. (1996). *Where Is Your Body? And Other Essays on Race, Gender and the Law.* Beacon Press.

Matsuda, M., Lawrence, C., Delgado, R., & Crenshaw, K. (1993). *Words that Wound: Critical Race Theory, Assaultive Speech, and the First Amendment.* Westview Press.

McRobbie, A. (2020). *Feminism and the Politics of Resilience: Essays on Gender, Media and the End of Welfare.* Polity Books.

Memon, A. R., & Jivraj, S. (2020). Trust, Courage and Silence: Carving Out Decolonial Spaces in Higher Education Through Student–Staff Partnerships. *The Law Teacher, 54*(4), 475–488.

Memon, A. R., & Olugboyega, J. (2020). Stripping the White Walls: The Podcast. In DecoloniseUoK Collective, D. Thomas, & S. Jivraj (Eds.), *Towards Decolonising the University: A Kaleidoscope for Empowered Action* (pp. 93–100). Counterpress.

Mignolo, W. D. (2009). Epistemic Disobedience, Independent Thought and Decolonial Freedom. *Theory, Culture and Society, 26*(7–8), 159–181.

Mignolo, W. D., & Vazquez, R. (2013, July 15). Decolonial AestheSis: Colonial Wounds/Decolonial Healings. *Social Text Online.* https://socialtextjournal.org/periscope_article/decolonial-aesthesis-colonial-woundsdecolonial-healings/

Mignolo, W. D., & Walsh, C. (2018). On Decoloniality. Concepts, Analytics, Praxis. In W. D. Mignolo & C. Walsh (Eds.), *On Decoloniality* (pp. 1–12). Duke University Press.

Miller, P. (2016). "White Sanction" Institutional, Group and Individual Interaction in the Promotion and Progression of Black and Minority Ethnic Academics and Teachers in England. *Power and Education, 8*(3), 205–221.

Mirza, H. S. (1997). *A Black British Feminism: A Reader*. Routledge.

Mirza, H. S. (2017). One in a Million: A Journey of a Post-colonial Woman of Colour in the White Academy. In S. A. Tate & D. Gabriel (Eds.), *Inside the Ivory Tower: Narratives of Women of Colour Surviving and Thriving in British Academia* (pp. 39–53). Trentham Books.

Mirza, H. S. (2018). Racism in Higher Education: What Then, Can Be Done? In J. Arday & H. S. Mirza (Eds.), *Dismantling Race in Higher Education: Racism, Whiteness and Decolonising the Academy* (pp. 1–7). Palgrave Macmillan.

Misra, A. (2020a). *Decolonising John Locke Walk*. Retrieved June 28, 2021, from https://research.kent.ac.uk/sergj/decolonising-john-locke/

Misra, A. (2020b). Decolonising Keynes: Between Memory and History. In DecoloniseUoK Collective, D. Thomas, & S. Jivraj (Eds.), *Towards Decolonising the University: A Kaleidoscope for Empowered Action* (pp. 33–47). Counterpress.

Morgan, W. (2016). *Why Is My Professor Still Not Black?* Retrieved June 28, 2021, from https://www.timeshighereducation.com/blog/why-my-professor-still-not-black

National Union of Students. (2016). *Why Is My Curriculum White? Decolonising the Academy*. Retrieved June 28, 2021, from https://www.nusconnect.org.uk/articles/why-is-my-curriculum-white-decolonising-the-academy

National Union of Students. (2021). *Decolonising Education: Decolonisers Festival*. Retrieved June 28, 2021, from https://www.nus.org.uk/campaigns/decolonising-education/decolonisers-programme

Office for Students. (2018). *Universities Must Eliminate Equality Gaps*. Retrieved July 12, 2021, from https://www.officeforstudents.org.uk/news-blog-and-events/press-and-media/office-for-students-universities-must-eliminate-equality-gaps/

Olufemi, L. (2019). Space. In L. Olufemi, O. Younge, W. Sebatindira, & S. Manzoor-Khan (Eds.), *A Fly Girl's Guide to University—Being a Woman of Colour at Cambridge and Other Institutions of Power and Elitism* (p. 119). Verve Poetry Press.

Owens, R. (2020). *Love and Rage: The Path of Liberation Through Anger*. North Atlantic Books.

Pilkington, A. (2013). The Interacting Dynamics of Institutional Racism in Higher Education. *Race Ethnicity and Education, 16*(2), 225–245.

Puwar, N. (2004). *Space Invaders: Race, Gender and Bodies Out of Place*. Berg.

Rhodes Must Fall Movement, Oxford (RMFO). (2018). *Rhodes Must Fall. The Struggle to Decolonise the Racist Heart of Empire*. Zed Books.

Rollock, N. (2016, January 19). How Much Does Your University Do for Racial Equality? *The Guardian*, London. Retrieved June 28, 2021, from https://www.theguardian.com/higher-education-network/2016/jan/19/how-much-does-your-university-do-for-racial-equality

Rollock, N. (2019). *Staying Power: The Career Experiences and Strategies of UK Black Female Professors*. University and College Union. Retrieved June 28, 2021, from https://www.ucu.org.uk/media/10075/Staying-Power/pdf/UCU_Rollock_February_2019.pdf

Rose, C. (1990). Property as Storytelling: Perspectives from Game Theory, Narrative Theory and Feminist Theory. *Yale Journal of Law and Humanities, 2*, 37–57.

Saini, A. (2019). *Superior: The Return of Race Science*. 4th Estate.

Shilliam, R. (2015). Black Academia: The Doors Have Been Opened But the Architecture Remains the Same. In C. Alexander & J. Arday (Eds.), *Aiming Higher: Race, Inequality and Diversity in the Academy* (pp. 32–34). Runnymede. Retrieved June 28, 2021, from https://www.runnymedetrust.org/uploads/Aiming Higher.pdf

Shoko, L. N. (2020). The Audacity to Occupy Spaces and Contribute to Knowledge. In DecoloniseUoK Collective, D. Thomas, & S. Jivraj (Eds.), *Towards Decolonising the University: A Kaleidoscope for Empowered Action* (pp. 143–149). Counterpress.

Sian, K. (2019). *Navigating Institutional Racism in British Universities*. Palgrave Macmillan.

SOAS. (2017). *Decolonising the Curriculum: What's All the Fuss About?* Retrieved June 28, 2021, from https://study.soas.ac.uk/decolonising-curriculum-whats-the-fuss/

Solórzano, D. G., & Yosso, T. J. (2002a). Critical Race Methodology: Counter-storytelling as an Analytical Framework for Education Research. *Qualitative Inquiry, 8*, 23–44.

Solórzano, D. G., & Yosso, T. J. (2002b). A Critical Race Counterstory of Race, Racism, and Affirmative Action. *Equity and Excellence in Education, 35*(2), 155–168.

Tate, S. A., & Bagguley, P. (2017). Building the Anti-racist University: Next Steps. *Race, Ethnicity and Education, 20*(3), 289–299.

Tate, S. A., & Page, D. (2018). Whiteliness and Institutional Racism: Hiding Behind (Un)Conscious Bias. *Ethics and Education, 13*(1), 141–155.

Tuck, E., & Yang, K. W. (2012). Decolonization Is Not a Metaphor. *Decolonization: Indigeneity, Education and Society, 1*(1), 1–40.

Tuck, E., & Yang, K. W. (2014). R-Words: Refusing Research. In D. Paris & M. T. Winn (Eds.), *Humanizing Research: Decolonizing Qualitative Inquiry with Youth and Communities*. Sage.

Tuhiwai Smith, L. (2012). *Decolonizing Methodologies: Research and Indigenous Peoples*. Zed Books.

Tuhiwai Smith, L., Tuck, E., & Yang, K. W. (Eds.). (2019). *Indigenous and Decolonizing Studies in Education*. Routledge.

UCLTV. (2014). *Why Isn't My Professor Black?* UCL Panel Discussion. https://www.youtube.com/watch?v=mBqgLK9dTk4

Williams, P. J. (1991). *The Alchemy of Race and Rights*. Harvard University Press.

Xaxa, A. (2011, September 19). I Am Not Your Data. *Roundtable India*. Retrieved June 28, 2021, from https://roundtableindia.co.in/lit-blogs/?tag=abhay-xaxa

Zahara, A. (2016, August 8). Ethnographic Refusal: A How to Guide. *Disabled Studies*. Retrieved June 28, 2021, from https://discardstudies.com/2016/08/08/ethnographic-refusal-a-how-to-guide/

Statutes

Higher Education and Research Act 2017.

CHAPTER 5

Exploring the Law/Bodies/Space Regulatory Conundrum

Helen Carr

Abstract This chapter explores the possibilities for a historically informed socio-legal engagement with law and the body in the context of the regulation of housing space. Its aim is to reveal what law obscures, the human body as it constitutes and is constituted by the law. The starting point is a moment in what I describe as a liminal legal space, when the interrelationship between law and the body is unexpectedly revealed. It then tracks the processes by which that moment might materialise as a coherent and theoretically informed piece of research, noting choices made, the influences upon those choices and the consequences, as well as the closures and deferrals which are an inevitable part of the research/writing trajectory. At the same time, the chapter seeks to acknowledge some of the practical/pragmatic realities of the writing/research process, not least editorial focus, and resource constraints. The chapter is not a blueprint for research but a tentative and personal reflection on the complexities of interdisciplinary socio-legal work.

Keywords Housing • Urban space • Inequality • Governance • Socio-legal • Liminality

H. Carr (✉)
University of Southampton, Southampton, UK
e-mail: h.p.carr@soton.ac.uk

D. Herman, C. Parsley (eds.), *Interdisciplinarities*, Palgrave Socio-Legal Studies, https://doi.org/10.1007/978-3-030-89297-5_5

Introduction

As a lawyer I lead a double life. I am a socio-legal scholar interested in housing and welfare and a part-time judge in the First-tier Tribunal (Property) Chamber (FTT). Most of the time—and probably quite rightly—these worlds are quite distinct. In one, I 'think like a lawyer', identifying facts and applying the law to those facts, disciplined by precedent, rules of evidence and the possibilities of appeal. In the other, I understand law as a social practice to be investigated and critiqued, relishing the 'many different points of view and disciplinary perspectives' that can be brought to bear (Lacey, 2017, p. 296). In any event, it can be difficult to connect decision-making about the reasonableness of individual service charges or the meaning of particular words of a lease, for instance (both major tasks of the FTT), with the more generalisable concerns and the creativity of socio-legal research. But sometimes it is fruitful to bring those worlds together, not least because academia frequently ignores the everyday work of low-level routine legal decision-making. And sometimes it just cannot be helped; the intellectual compartmentalisation breaks down as the contradictions and complexities of applying law in books to the materiality of life become unavoidable. The request to contribute to an edited collection on bodies recalled one of those latter moments when the familiarity of applying legal rules suddenly and inadvertently became strange (Garfinkel, 1967), and the complex relationship between the body and the law, so often covert, became overt. In this chapter, I will track the origins of that moment and the processes by which that moment might materialise as a coherent piece of research. Two caveats from the outset; choices made about what not to do and what avenues not to follow are as important as the active research choices, although often more difficult to articulate and, despite the structure of this chapter, any suggestion that the process is linear rather than iterative is misleading. For these reasons, I have made my account open, revealing the points where choices could be made and exploring the potential consequences of those choices.

The Productivity of a Liminal Legal Space

The moment when I suddenly and unexpectedly saw the intimate relationship between bodies and law was neither in the courtroom nor in the legal texts. It was in what, on reflection, is best described as a liminal legal space. The notion of liminality, derived from anthropology, refers to a status of in-betweenness and uncertainty which can be applied to people, communities, or spaces. Legal liminality/liminal legality has been explored by scholars such as Desmond Manderson (2005) and Jennifer Chacon (2015) and drawn upon, for instance, in analyses of immigration status, international law and war zones. The legal liminality in which I found myself is more domestic. The tribunal has a power to inspect property that is the subject of proceedings in the presence of the parties. On reflection it is quite an extraordinary power. Judges and property professionals go into people's homes to see the material realities of the case they are considering, to ask tenants to point out to them, to give one example, the reasons why the rent demanded by the landlord is not fair, or in other circumstances to see for themselves why the property might be considered a fire risk. This creates a liminal legal space—one that is neither a courtroom nor the home it was prior to the entry of the law. When the tribunal inspects, it brings with it legal hierarchies and formalities and disturbs what is familiar. On the other hand, the law is only a transitory presence in the home and its status is uncertain. It has to be invited in and that invitation can be withdrawn, and it has to listen to stories of the home that might not conform to its legal understandings. The ambiguous status of inspections enables interventions which can be unexpected and revealing, particularly as occupiers or owners reassert their control of the space. What it also reveals is the juxtaposition of the domestic, the material and the corporeal and the law.

The incident that came to mind when asked to think about bodies was this: I, along with two colleagues from the tribunal, was inspecting a bed-sitting room in an HMO—a house in multiple occupation, a technical label for shared housing in the UK—in prosperous central London. The landlord was challenging the local authority decision that the room was too small to be rented out. The room was attractive and well lit, but small and particularly narrow. There was a matchbox kitchen area at one end of the room with the rest of the length of the room taken up with a bed settee. The combined bathroom and WC was just outside of the room and shared with other occupiers of the house. I said something without really thinking about it, that I had noticed that if you opened the bed settee you would not be able to open the door of the room to access the toilet. The landlord replied: 'What we find is that the young men who rent these rooms tend to only put up the bed settee when their girlfriends are round. Otherwise, they just sleep on the settee without opening it up.' My question and the response suddenly made clear to me the corporeal implications of the decision we were making. The rules about how big a room has to be before it can be rented out directly impact upon the way people manage their bodies in their domestic space. At the same time, those rules provide an interesting example of how law is required to acknowledge, however minimally, the functional requirements of the body. The law only intervenes at the margins, at a point when the space is on the verge of becoming too small, but it is at that vanishing point when the interrelationship between law and the body becomes visible. We learn something important about how law, as a tool of the state, imagines/constructs the body and how the body compels and shapes legal/state interventions. It was that moment that came back to me when asked to think about the body, the concrete moment when it became apparent how the corporeal constitutes and is constituted by technical legal rules. It chimed with other experiences of thinking about domestic space, how, for instance, untidiness is made problematic even when the living space provided is very small. So, for example, when a landlord is confronted by photographs of a small room cluttered with belongings and trailing laptop wires, he conjures up a previous occupier who kept the room in pristine condition—a chef, apparently, who worked 12 hours a day, kept the tools of his trade at work, and in effect only used the room to sleep. The ideal occupier of contemporary micro-spaces, it appears, has the body of a disciplined asexual worker. But at the same time the law is providing some resistance to this economic reductionism of the body, acknowledging, however conditionally, its social, sexual, physical and emotional dimensions.

The exchange with the landlord provided a potential starting point for my research on bodies. However, experience tells me that it is not enough to have a thought that captures my imagination; it must have sufficient substance and resonance to merit a research focus and provide an opportunity to make an original contribution. Otherwise, it can be jettisoned or filed away somewhere until it becomes more relevant.

Looking for the Body (1): Scanning the Scene

For me, a next step in a research project is to ask questions about my starting point to help me appreciate the broader context. This is not a formal literature review, which can wait until my research questions are more concrete. Rather it is a scoping of the terrain, a gleaning of knowledge and an identification of contestations. So, for instance, in the context of the state's project to regulate domestic space, how, if at all, are different stakeholders thinking about the body? How is the body made visible and/or problematised? What is at stake about the body for the different parties, including the state? Is it the health of the body, for instance, or its social/sexual/economic functioning? Who wins and who loses from the current position? What I am looking for are answers that reveal complexities and contradictions and provide an opportunity to think against the grain. Ideally, I want the research and writing process to be intellectually exciting and, at the end of that process, to think differently from my starting point. So, for instance, I have little interest in pursuing questions about whether occupiers would prefer bigger rooms and more facilities—the answer to this must surely be yes. Even at this initial stage I am looking for the potential for something more complex to emerge. What is attractive about an analytical/conceptual focus on the body is that it should facilitate exactly that. This is important because social welfare law resists acknowledging and accommodating the body, even though bodies—particularly those of the poor and vulnerable—are central to its concerns. It shares with social policy what Julia Twigg describes as an 'absent presence' of the body (Twigg, 2002).

Interrogating technical law is an important part of my scholarship reflecting my interest in law as a practice or technique of government (Dean, 2009). This can be problematic as I can sometimes be rather too pleased with my own mastery of the complexities of the law and produce a 'law first' account. Nonetheless, reviewing the law is an important step in understanding the context and, hopefully, keeping the body in mind ensures a proper perspective. There is no simple answer in English law to the question about minimum room sizes. It depends upon the context, so questions of overcrowding are resolved differently from minimum room size requirements for HMOs (but there are no such requirements for other private rentals) and then differently again within planning requirements for new developments. The body is generally invisible in the legal rules, although the Housing Health and Safety Rating System (HHSRS), which applies across tenures and is used to manage health and safety risks in homes, does consider the body. It recognises lack of space and crowding as a hazard which is linked to 'psychological distress and various mental disorders. It is also linked to increased heart rate, increased perspiration, intolerance, inability to concentrate, hygiene risks, accidents and spread of contagious disease' (Department for Communities and Local Government (DCLG), 2006, p. 35). This means that, where local housing authorities assess these risks to be high, they can, and on occasions must, take enforcement action.

The legal regimes are quite distinct, although there seems to be some sort of consensus that individual bodies require around 6.5 square metres of living space. This standard was set in the overcrowding provisions of the Housing Act 1935 and has not been updated. It is important not to overstate that consensus and to recognise that the regulation of space is contentious (Wilson & Barton, 2020). In response to a controversial Upper Tribunal decision,[1] for instance, the government was prepared to prescribe a national minimum room size of 6.51 square metres for houses in multiple occupation where none existed before (DCLG, 2018). In contrast, and as part of a deregulation drive, it abandoned local authority-imposed minimum size standards for new developments (DCLG, 2015). The political contestations around housing space were made most visible by the 'bedroom tax', the informal label attached by opponents to the cuts to housing benefit payments to social tenants with more bedrooms than overcrowding standards prescribed. This was justified by politicians by claims of fairness in the allocation of space between those renting in the social and private sectors, as well as the need to reduce overcrowding (Carr & Cowan, 2015). Calls for political and legal interventions on housing space may well resurface as evidence grows of a correlation between Covid-19 infections and cramped and overcrowded housing.

The body does not appear to feature in the policy debates on room sizes and overcrowding, although there are relatively extensive discussions about the impact of overcrowding on children's education (see, for instance, Hansard, 2003 for a typical example).[2] Arguably, the fixation with numbers becomes a proxy for the body. More is made of the physical implications of overcrowding by Shelter as it seeks to influence policy development. It worked via discussion groups, workshops, and quantitative surveys to gather public views on what a home should provide, developing what it calls a Living Home Standard (Shelter, 2016). The conclusions on space were that there needed to be an adequate number of bedrooms, sufficient space to allow everyone privacy, adequate storage, and adequate space to prepare and cook food. The research

[1] *Clark v Manchester City Council* [2015] UKUT 0129.

[2] HC Deb 22 January 2003, vol. 398, cols 323–325.

revealed that people primarily thought about their space needs in terms of functional and social requirements. There was also an interesting suggestion that people were prepared to trade off space for affordability.

It is not easy to find a focus in this rather messy context, but points have begun to emerge which capture my interest; concern about room sizes is not tenure-specific unlike most housing law issues. There is a strong but contested correlation between the housing crisis and the availability of housing space (see Dorling, 2014; and the Institute of Economic Affairs' response from Niemietz, 2014), and I can see that incoherence in regulation might provide opportunities to challenge discourse dominated by the market and to interrogate the role of law in resisting the economic invisibilisation of the body that I identified earlier. Nonetheless, academic interest in housing space is limited. Tunstall's work provides a notable exception. Her interest is the politics of housing space distribution. Her analysis demonstrates that, for those years of the twentieth century when council housing was being built,

> housing space inequality, or low relative consumption of housing space, fell markedly, for most of the period. However, from 1981 or 1991, housing space inequality started to increase again, and by 2011, by some measures, this new trend had wiped out a century's worth of reductions in inequality. (2015, p. 105)

I can see that this work is likely to provide a useful foundation for my own approach. It chimes with Dorling's more polemical arguments on housing inequalities (Dorling, 2015). It provides a counternarrative to the more dominant account of council housing as social policy failure. And law is missing, so I can add something of interest.

But of course, and significantly, the body is also missing. I need other sources to reinvigorate my initial insight into the important but overlooked interrelationship between the body, the home and the law. The media demonstrates a much greater interest in bodies forced into cramped housing than policy or academic work. Britain's 'rabbit hutch homes' regularly hit the headlines (see, for instance, Brown, 2014; Jones, 2017), the metaphor suggesting that these rooms do not provide enough space to allow people to function as human. Media interest in the alleged proliferation of 'beds in sheds' (Foster, 2014) also invokes the body, but there are racial overtones—landlords (frequently BAME) are accused of cramming foreigners into squalid conditions (Harvey, 2017). This brings David Nelken's seminal work on landlord crime to mind, and perhaps the current re-regulation of the private rented sector provides an opportunity to revisit his research into the disproportionate enforcement of housing laws against migrant landlords (Nelken, 2013, 2020; Carr & Alcock, 2020). Something else captures my imagination; searching for news items on Google I learn from the *Oxford Mail*, that

> A plane flying over the streets of Oxford has helped catch dozens of rogue landlords keeping tenants in 'appalling' conditions in garden sheds.

> The aircraft has used a thermal imaging camera to spot the illegal structures where often vulnerable people are charged to live in cramped squalor. (Ffrench, 2019)

Here is a whole new dimension to explore—the detectability of body heat in buildings leading to a potentially new configuration of a perennially interesting line of housing scholarship, the policies and practices of surveillance, technologies and policing (Flint, 2003; Carr et al., 2007). This is not a direction I want to take now; it is too remote from the everyday legalities and the co-constitution of the law and the body that I want to focus on. However, it may well be a productive line of enquiry in the future, perhaps for a paper where technology is a significant focus.

I also try to gather insights from my love of literary fiction. Victorian literature is full of accounts of squalid housing packed with undernourished and diseased bodies. Dickens, for instance, uses the inadequacies of urban housing to provide an essential backdrop to his 'condition of England'[3] novels, such as *Hard Times*, *Bleak House* and *Little Dorrit*. In contemporary literature, the urban crisis and the disparities between those with property and those without frequently play an important role. In the critically acclaimed *Luster* (Leilani, 2021), for instance, Edie, the young black woman at the centre of the story, is precariously employed in publishing. Her financial insecurity means that she flat-shares in New York; it is squalid, infested with mice and roaches, not somewhere that she can take her married lover without acute embarrassment. When her job goes, she loses even this inadequate housing, and rather disturbingly ends up in the family home of her lover, a stylish and spacious house in a white suburb.[4] Usefully for this piece, *Luster* exemplifies one of the strengths of contemporary literature. Bodies alive and dead are central to its concerns. The protagonist's painting of her mother's body following a fatal overdose haunts the novel. Her lover's wife dissects dead bodies and encourages Edie to paint her at work. And throughout the novel there is a particular voyeurism, bodies and bodily functions, including copulation are observed, recorded and reflected as if somehow being seen, even if only by yourself, is the only proof of existence. Clearly, there is a distinction between fiction and the socio-legal, and I have sympathy with Twigg's observation that academic work concerning the body can be voyeuristic with the potential to demean and diminish (Twigg, 2004). Nonetheless, the assertion of the importance and indeed unavoidability of the corporeal that *Luster* provides is a necessary correction to its absence from legal and policy discourse.

There are three other points that *Luster* raises that may be worth exploration; first, young people may well want or need to live in the centre of cities.

[3] 'Condition of England' was a term coined by Thomas Carlyle in 1839 to describe novels concerned with social problems and the need for reform. See 'The Condition of England Novel' (Ratcliffe, 2014).

[4] For another example, see *Hot Stew* by Fiona Mozley (2021) which tells a story of sex workers' resistance to property development in contemporary Soho.

Despite the hardships, Edie welcomes her return to the city—she prefers its diversity and its food, and it is of course better located for the insecure work that she, like so many, relies on. So young people may be prepared to sacrifice space for the benefits of a diverse, convenient, or fashionable location and resent regulation that restricts its provision. At the FTT, it is notable how very few tenants object to the size of rooms—one landlord told us that when tenants in his shared houses had the opportunity to upgrade, they chose en suite facilities rather than bigger rooms. There may or may not be evidence to support this, but it is important to remember it as a possibility that for some people at certain periods in their lives, room size may be far less important than location. Second, activities that might in the past have taken place in the privacy of the home are, for those who live in small, shared spaces, in effect contracted out. So sexual encounters take place in hotel rooms and cafes, and coffee shops become sites for the performance of friendship and intimacy. There are undoubtedly interesting consequences to this commodification of social relations and their performance in the liminal spaces of commercial hospitality, as well as of course the impact of the curtailing of these opportunities because of Covid-19 restrictions. *Luster* provides a third related insight. Edie relies on storage units to store her personal possessions when she is evicted. I have noticed how storage units are now explicitly marketed at people living in small and/or shared housing. There is something quite intriguing about considering the impact upon our identities and our homes when our possessions are dispersed in this way. Whilst this suggests a tempting deviation from the chapter that is beginning to take shape in my mind—and it is reassuring to see how productive the relationship between housing space, bodies and the law is proving to be—I need to remind myself to focus. A chapter in an edited collection can only cover so much ground.

Already my scan of the broader legal and policy context informed by my own experience and my literary encounters nudges me into a more conceptual questioning of the contemporary urban body. This enhances the possibility of making a distinctive socio-legal contribution over and beyond a straightforward exposition of the law. But first there is a need to impose some sort of coherence and direction on the information and policy insights I have gathered.

Conceptualising the Problem

Faced with an undoubtedly messy terrain, choices must be made about how to organise the materials I have gleaned and the appropriate conceptual framework for the questions I want to ask. My possible approaches, which build upon previous research, are distinct though interlinked. I could start by thinking about the relationship between law and the meaning of home for people who are marginally housed, or I could start with the politics of the regulation of people's homes. The focus on the body brings a real possibility of an important reinvigoration of both of these approaches.

The first approach has an empirical and/or doctrinal orientation, suggesting questions about how law actually functions in reality and the actors that shape its implementation. Here the body could provide an important focus for my explorations of how rules on room sizes operate as constraints and resistance. The second is more theoretical, raising conceptual questions about the relationship between law and society and drawing more broadly on sociology history and politics (O'Donovan, 2016). In this instance, how law imagines and accommodates the body and how the messy realities of bodily life impact upon the law will be important.

The first approach could take as its starting point work on law and home primarily articulated by Lorna Fox who argues that law ought to recognise and protect the status of home in a coherent and principled way (Fox, 2007). This is innovative and important work at perhaps the socio-legal edge of the doctrinal, but I have some doubts about its appropriateness for this proposed project. I have a feminist concern with the potential of privileging an idealised notion of home rather than revealing its inherent contradictions and the tensions between security/insecurity, freedom/constraint and so on, which are encapsulated in home as a concept. In addition, whilst Fox focuses on property law and the owner-occupied home, for me, it is the contribution that law makes to the precarity of many people's homes, regardless of tenure and property law, that is more interesting and productive, and I am not convinced that her work is sufficiently attentive to the issues I wish to explore (Carr et al., 2018). I am also concerned that there are serious limits in a project which requires law to value the subjective and contested space of the home, when law's logic is quite different. Its rules are designed to promote certainty and objectivity, and any recognition it might give to the subjective and contested space of the home can, in my opinion, seldom be more than peripheral. More recently, I have become interested in home as a continuous and messy process which involves practices of making, unmaking and remaking (Baxter & Brickell, 2014), and in particular how law might become implicated in and impact upon that process (Carr & Meers, 2022). There may be some mileage in developing this approach, and I explore below what this might look like methodologically as well as its potential as a feminist legal heuristic. There is a problem though. Can I persuade the editors of the collection that home making/unmaking/remaking is a sufficiently corporeal process? My answer would be that making/unmaking/remaking home inevitably involves physical processes. Jeremy Waldron put this elegantly in his seminal essay on homelessness and freedom.

> Everything that is done has to be done somewhere. No one is free to perform an action unless there is somewhere he is free to perform it. Since we are embodied beings, we always have a location. (Waldron, 1991)

The connection that Waldron makes between freedom and embodied location is also significant, reminding us that the body is more than its physical functioning, but also includes social relations and ways of being. Exploring the relationship between the body and its location in the context of small room sizes empirically via home making/unmaking/remaking may not only provide substance to Waldron's deliberately abstract analysis but also offer productive insights into the relationship between law and the performance of embodiment in the home.

My alternative approach is to respond to and extend Tunstall's insight that the distribution of housing space is political by bringing the body more consciously into play. There is a clear tension between the politics of welfare, which values housing space as a good, and the politics of the market, which valorises the individual exercising freedoms. The latter has become dominant over the last thirty years and this, as Tunstall's work demonstrates, has had consequences. Yet, however, dominant contractual norms are, the regulation of room sizes continues, representing a departure from free market logics and a reminder that alternative politics have not been eliminated but continue to have potency. In certain circumstances, society will step in to protect people from the consequences of the market. This resonates with Polanyi's 'double movement' thesis (Polanyi, 2001) and provides the possibility of exploring the regulation of room sizes in Polanyian terms as a 'countermovement', a mechanism to engage the state in resisting the expansion of the market. I have explored elsewhere the productive overlaps between Polanyian and legal thinking drawing on Patrick Atiyah's seminal work *The Rise and Fall of Freedom of Contract* (1979) (Carr & Alcock, 2020). But in this project, using Polanyi as a conceptual framing may prove problematic because of the need for a focus on the body. In a way not untypical of a mid-twentieth-century male thinker, Polanyi says little about the body, even in the context of manual labour, something with which he is very much concerned. It may be more productive to take a lead from Edward Kirton-Darling who, in a thoughtful and prescient paper on the inadequacies of government responses to deaths in a fire at Lakanal House in 2009, draws upon theoretical work on precariousness to frame his analysis (Kirton-Darling, 2018). The body, he observes, drawing on Judith Butler (2004, 2010), is inevitably 'vulnerable to the activities of anonymous others, rendering impossible claims of absolute control and protection' (2018, p. 182). He also tracks precarity as a governance technique, the move from liberal governmental use of precarity as a form of exclusion/inclusion, the protection of some and the construction of the dangerous other, to neoliberal governance which relies on insecurity as a normalised mode of governing, shifts identified by Isabell Lorey (2015), but to which Kirton-Darling adds substance through his analysis of social housing in England and Wales. However, whilst the work on precariousness is persuasive, and there is no doubt that the proliferation of living in small spaces is intimately connected to economic precarisation, as *Luster* illustrated, I am concerned that it might be too brutal and blunt a tool. Living in small spaces is much more mundane than the careless governance of the fire risks of multi-occupied buildings. It is its very mundaneness that I find attractive because I want to reveal that everyday existence is as important, perplexing and vivid as the exotic or the extreme.

Moreover, occupiers have some agency. There is evidence of their resistance to the prohibition of small living spaces, and the existence of low-level regulatory enforcement suggests that social protections persist. Work on precarity, however, is very close to governmentality theory, and this is what I consider next.

Governmentality is my preferred tool for revealing how the body figures in the politics of housing space. Drawing on the work of Michel Foucault (1991) and developed by academics such as Nikolas Rose (1999) and Mitchell Dean (2009), my expectation is that governmentality scholarship will provide some insight into how working-class bodies have been and continue to be imagined and indeed problematised by law, via the spaces in which they live and work. Governmentality retains the historical perspective of Polanyi, but through its interest in biopolitics it makes clear the long-standing relationship between technologies of social welfare law and the bodies of the working poor. It has a tradition of interest in public health as a means of governing populations (Foucault, 1991; Osborne, 2005) perhaps best exemplified by Christopher Hamlin's critique of Chadwick's sanitary laws, often presented as foundational in any history of liberal social intervention (Hamlin, 1998). There is something else as well: living in small spaces inculcates particular habits of self-discipline, of tidiness and constraint that resonates with governmentality's concern with governing through freedom and the conduct of conduct. Governmentality does not shy away from the mundane, something as ordinary as the emergence of the storage unit can be understood, for instance, as a form of conduct of conduct. Storage units provide the possibility for both consumption and constraint, a requirement of the neoliberal urban economy. Governmentality will also provide an opportunity to reflect quite carefully upon what Ross Exo describes as the urbanization of the body, a product, he argues, of the distinct and contemporary phenomenon of the emergence of the urban as a spatio-political order (Exo, 2015). Although critiques of the correlation between the neoliberal and the urban are persuasive, I have some concern that they frequently pay insufficient attention to the spatial conditions of everyday practices and to agency and resistance. I am interested in decentred theory as a brake on the metanarratives of governmentality. Developed by Mark Bevir and Roderick Rhodes (2001), what it provides for me is a potentially more nuanced approach to the practices of the state, seeing it not simply as a monolith that promotes market logics but as something more complex. It requires that attention is paid to the actions, contingent beliefs and diverse traditions of individual social actors (Bevir, 2013, 2016). This may enable me to disentangle, for instance, the role of environmental health officers from what might otherwise be a teleological account of the state.

Looking for the Body (2): Methods

A next step is to consider the methods that I might use to gather data in any project I pursue to make the relationship between the body, the law and room sizes visible.

Gathering Empirical Data

If I decide to explore more fully the relationship between law and the meaning of home for people who are housed in small spaces, this might, as I indicated above, suggest an empirical project. Semi-structured interviews and focus groups will provide an opportunity to pay close attention to the everyday realities of living in small spaces. Inspired in part by *Luster*, questions can be asked about the use of space, the physical compromises that people make, and what impact this might have on their intimate lives and on their identities. The relationship between the choices people make and their gender, class, ethnicity and sexuality could be examined. It might also be possible to explore any trade-offs between location, space and affordability. It would be interesting to discover whether certain functions of the home, such as social activities or storage of personal possessions, are in effect dispersed or contracted out, to see whether commercial spaces are used to provide necessary extensions to domestic space. Alternatively, it may be that small living spaces are made possible because of extensive reliance on parental housing space, so that relationships with the family home are more prolonged than might have been expected. This might highlight important differentials between those with and those without financial and familial resources and the constraints imposed by small home spaces. There may be difficulties in accessing research participants, but house-share websites would provide a useful resource, Shelter may be prepared to advertise the research project, and, once some participants are identified, no doubt a snowball approach will recruit others.

This data could be complemented by locating local authority decisions under the HHSRS to see how often enforcement action is initiated under the space hazard, and with what success, and the tribunal website could be checked to see how often landlords appeal and with what results. Finally, there may be the opportunity for a more extensive empirical project, working perhaps alongside psychology, architecture and health studies academics. The aim would be to gather data on the harms that are experienced by those living in overcrowded conditions—the current guidance indicates that there is limited evidence of harm.

Enriching Legal Analysis

The second method I might use is quite experimental. My aim would be to develop home making/unmaking/remaking as an interpretive lens to reveal some of the presumptions of decision makers regarding bodies in their homes and to investigate possibilities for different legal rulings—a form of 'academic activism' not so far removed from the Feminist Judgments Project (Hunter et al., 2010). Bringing embodiment and location into play with home as a process might stimulate a progressive pluralisation of legal understandings of home (Feldman, 2004) which could be emancipatory for those who are excluded from conventional approaches such as the homeless, victims of domestic abuse or the young people described as 'generation rent' because of what looks like a permanent exclusion from owner occupation. For an example of how this might work, I draw on *Nottingham City Council v Parr*,[5] a Supreme Court case concerned with room sizes in two student HMOs. This is not the place to explore the technical legal provisions, interesting though I find them. What is relevant are the rationales used by the different courts to justify decisions that the council was unable to prohibit the use of attic bedrooms, despite the useable floor surface being less than 8 square metres, its own minimum room size. Exploiting the flexibility built into the guidance, the FTT concluded that the attic rooms were adequate as study/bedrooms in housing 'where cohesive living is envisaged' because the provision of communal living space was significantly larger than the minimum suggested by Nottingham's guidance and therefore compensated for the small size of the bedrooms. It took steps, however, to limit occupation of the properties to students. The Upper Tribunal (Lands Chamber) rejected Nottingham's appeal, agreeing with the FTT that there was something distinct about student properties where communal living and social interaction was envisioned. The Court of Appeal and the Supreme Court substantially agreed. Delivering the unanimous decision, Lord Lloyd-Jones explained that the Supreme Court considered it to be,

> entirely appropriate, when considering the suitability of accommodation in an HMO for a particular purpose, to have regard to the mode of occupation. If a house is to be occupied by a group living together 'cohesively', each having his or her own bedroom but sharing other facilities including a kitchen/diner and a living room, the availability of those additional facilities is a material consideration … the shared facilities will benefit all the occupants and, as a result, this may compensate for a bedroom which is slightly smaller than the recommended minimum.… [25]

There is potentially more to this dispute than a conflict between the economic and contractual concerns of the tribunal and courts and the council's focus on housing as social protection. My suggestion is that if we interrogate the decisions using notions of home making/unmaking and remaking, we can uncover some of the assumptions being made by the decision makers and identify those interests that are made invisible or peripheral. So, for instance, the FTT marginalises the social and functional concerns of the local authority who were concerned throughout the legal proceedings to assert the significance of universal social provision and avoid the creation of a category of occupiers who could be provided with lower standards of accommodation than others. The FTT also appears to have based its decision on a notion of home making by students that replicates the cohesiveness of the family life they are presumed to have left behind. But, arguably, this ignores the home making—and unmaking—practices of students who are frequently forced to band together based on

[5] [2018] UKSC 51.

recently formed social bonds to look collectively for a shared house at the same time as they are emerging as independent adults with complex social, sexual and economic relationships. It is at this point it may be productive to refer to the insights about the lives of young people that I draw from *Luster* and other contemporary literature as a useful counterweight to the perspective of the judges whose experience as students is not only long ago but qualitatively different in very many ways.

The research project would provide an opportunity to work out this method more fully, to consider what legal decisions it might encompass and what the final conclusions might be. It may be that it has the potential to be useful beyond the current regulatory framework, perhaps providing a way to reimagine the regulation of room sizes that avoids a crude implementation of social protection and engages more carefully with the aspirations, compromises and well-being of those who are meant to be the beneficiaries of the rules.

A Genealogical Approach

The third method I might consider—genealogy—is more established. It derives from a theoretical commitment to governmentality and seeks to provide an explanation of the present which avoids grounding it in a metanarrative of progress. It identifies and characterises concerns that have emerged relatively recently, as well as the continuities in problematisations between the past and the present. For Dean, genealogy is, in brief,

> The patient labour of historico-political analysis and a contestation of existing narratives. It is animated by a particular ethos of permanent and pragmatic activism without apocalyptic or messianic ends. (2009, p. 61)

Exploring the contingent and contested ways in which the rules on room sizes emerged and how the law constitutes and is constituted by particular understandings of the body would be more of a micro-project of genealogy, or perhaps it is better described as an archaeology—a careful un-layering of the currently existing law. It is made possible because of the relatively short history of laws restraining the provision of too small spaces of living and working—a history that coincides with the urbanisation and industrialisation of the United Kingdom. The Housing Act 1935 will provide an interesting start. Room sizes were not the main concern of the legislation. Its primary focus was slum clearance, a necessary first step in a project of creating modern cities and nations. However, the government was forced to include within the legislation provisions that set standards for room sizes that are still in use. The legislation contained something unique, a statement that the 'standard does not represent any ideal standard of housing, but the minimum which is in the view of Parliament tolerable while at the same time capable of immediate or early enforcement' (Memorandum B Housing Act 1935). Compromise and contestation are therefore in full view on the face of the statute which suggests that a more careful interrogation of the debates around the legislation may well be productive.

In addition, there is the lure of following the numbers. From what evidence did 6.5 square metres emerge? What is the knowledge base for their survival to the present? There are no readily available explanations. However, Benjamin Seebohm Rowntree's ground-breaking work of empirical sociology, *Poverty: A Study of Town Life*, published in 1901, contains a useful reference to *The Theory and Practice of Hygiene* (Notter & Firth, 1894) in which, as Rowntree informs us, the question of the air space required for health purposes is fully discussed (Rowntree, 1901, p. 172) providing a first step for a genealogical inquiry. There is also something to explore in the emergence of space requirements imposed by the Victorians on common lodging houses which were understood to be a health risk because of the immorality of the occupants. Perhaps most intriguing of all are the possible connections between contemporary regulation of room sizes and the rules governing the size of barracks (Parkes, 1866) imposed following the Crimean War in which the poor conditions of military accommodation were responsible for more deaths than the battlefields. Establishing a connection between those rules and the contemporary rules on room sizes would enable interesting conclusions about liberal governance, about whose bodies are to be protected and why, and the circumstances when prevailing doctrines of the free market and self-reliance might be disapplied. Literature is an invaluable resource for my genealogical project. I will explore the extent to which Victorian novelists' concern with social conscience and the need for an ideal landlord to house the poor impacted upon and explained the emergent law, as well as the influence of early twentieth-century technological optimism and its links with social progress, so ably satirised by Aldous Huxley in *Brave New World*. So, Sir William Beveridge, for instance, called upon the architect to be the Lord Shaftsbury of the home,

> That means thinking not only of the walls or roof or the shape and size of the rooms but of every detail of equipment and its placing. That means thinking of how to make homes not only well but quickly and cheaply. (Beveridge, 1943, p. 172)

He continues by making explicit the links between technical improvements and the quality—and quantity—of the population.

> it is important also that those who design houses today should realise that they must be birthplaces of the Britons of the future—of more Britons than are being born today. (Beveridge, 1943, p. 172)

This provides a stark reminder that the regulation of bodies in their homes is not inevitably benign.

Conclusion

It has been an interesting exercise to write what is in effect simultaneously a prelude to a piece of research and a reflection on the research process. Tracking my ways of thinking through something from a glimmer of an idea to something more concrete but not yet fully realised has been a challenge, particularly because ideas emerge in a multiplicity of ways. Moreover, the act of writing is in itself a significant way to make my thoughts concrete and complete. I find the closure that promises hard to resist, but it can lead to me overstating processes which may be much more tentative and fluid than they appear. Overall, my aim has been to share insights into what Nelken describes as the 'often "messy" circumstances of scientific production' (Nelken, 2013, p. 2), but I am rather concerned that the mess is all too apparent whilst its productiveness less so.

Nonetheless, there are some points that are worth highlighting. Firstly, the richness and diversity of socio-legal research is apparent—there are clearly many ways in which a socio-legal researcher can investigate and think about the body. Secondly, it is important to recognise the close connections between theory and method: they are not distinct ways of thinking but inevitably interlinked, and both should permeate research practices. Thirdly, it was not easy to keep the body visible in work which is socio-legal because of the pull of the law. I had consciously to remind myself of the brief and avoid getting immersed in more abstract analysis. For a social welfare scholar, the problem of the abject body highlighted by Twigg should always be borne in mind. The public information films produced in the mid-twentieth century about slum clearance demonstrate the problem. No doubt the producers were keen to broadcast the value of social interventions, but highlighting squalid homes, infestations and ill-nourished bodies is very demeaning of those whose lot was supposed to be improved (see Hackney, 1935 for an example). Finally, all suggestions about how to proceed must recognise the contemporary realities of scholarship. We must be pragmatic about what we can achieve and take careful account of available resources, including time.

References

Atiyah, P. S. (1979). *The Rise and Fall of Freedom of Contract.* Oxford University Press.

Baxter, R., & Brickell, K. (2014). For Home UnMaking. *Home Cultures: Journal of Architecture, Design and Domestic Space, 18*(2), 133–143.

Beveridge, W. (1943). *The Pillars of Security and Other Wartime Essays and Addresses.* George Allen & Unwin.

Bevir, M. (2013). *A Theory of Governance.* University of California Press.

Bevir, M. (2016). *Governmentality after Neoliberalism.* In M. Bevir (Ed.), *Governmentality after Neoliberalism.* Routledge.

Bevir, M., & Rhodes, R. (2001). Decentering Tradition: Interpreting British Government. *Administration and Society, 33*(2), 107–132.

Brown, J. (2014). Rabbit-hutch Britain: Growing Health Concerns as UK Sets Record for Smallest Properties in Europe. *The Independent*, 18 June.

Butler, J. (2004). *Precarious Life: The Powers of Mourning and Violence*. Verso.

Butler, J. (2010). *Frames of War: When Is Life Grievable?* Verso.

Carr, H., & Alcock, R. (2020). Understanding the (Re-)regulation of Private Renting in England: Karl Polanyi, the Rogue Landlord, the Responsible Tenant and the Decent Home. In T. T. Arvind & J. Steele (Eds.), *Contract Law and the Legislature: Autonomy, Expectations, and the Making of Legal Doctrine*. Hart.

Carr, H., & Cowan, D. (2015). The Social Tenant, the Law and the UK's Politics of Austerity. *Oñati Socio-legal Series, 5*, 73–89.

Carr, H., Cowan, D., & Hunter, C. (2007). Policing the Housing Crisis. *Critical Social Policy, 27*(1), 100–127.

Carr, H., Edgeworth, B., & Hunter, C. (2018). Introduction. In H. Carr, B. Edgeworth, & C. Hunter (Eds.), *Law and the Precarious Home: Socio-Legal Perspectives on the Home in Insecure times*. Hart.

Carr, H., & Meers, J. (2022). "A Homemaker as well as a Judge": Lady Hale and judicial homemaking/unmaking/remaking. In R. Hunter & E. Rackley (Eds.), *Justice for Everyone: The Jurisprudence and Legal Lives of Brenda Hale*. Cambridge University Press.

Chacon, J. M. (2015). Producing Liminal Legality. *Denver University Law Review, 92*, 709.

Dean, M. (2009 [1999]). *Governmentality: Power and Rule in Modern Society*. Sage.

Department for Communities and Local Government (DCLG). (2006). Housing Health and Safety Rating System: Guidance for Landlords and Property Related Professionals.

Department for Communities and Local Government (DCLG). (2015). Technical Housing Standards: Nationally Described Space Standard.

Department for Communities and Local Government (DCLG). (2018). The Licensing of Houses in Multiple Occupation (Mandatory Conditions of Licences) (England) Regulations 2018.

Dorling, D. (2014). *All that Is Solid: The Great Housing Disaster* (Kindle ed.). Penguin.

Dorling, D. (2015). Policy, Politics, Health and Housing in the UK. *Policy and Politics, 43*(2), 163–180.

Exo, R. (2015). Ubiquitous Law and the Urbanisation of the Body (draft paper presented at Thinking Spatial Practices within and against Law, Birkbeck Institute of Social Research). Retrieved June 25, 2021, from https://www.academia.edu/13237483/Ubiquitous_Law_and_the_Urbanisation_of_the_Body

Feldman, L. (2004). *Citizens without Shelter: Homelessness, Democracy and Political Exclusion*. Cornell University Press.

Ffrench, A. (2019). Oxford City Council Uses Infrared Plane to Find Beds in Sheds. *Oxford Mail*, 29 August. Retrieved June 25, 2021, from https://www.oxfordmail.co.uk/news/17867233.oxford-city-council-uses-infrared-plane-find-beds-sheds

Flint, J. (2003). Housing and Ethopolitics: Constructing Identities of Active Consumption and Responsible Community. *Economy and Society, 32*(4), 611–629.

Foster, D. (2014). Beds in Sheds Show who the Real Victims of the Housing Crisis Are. *The Guardian*, 1 July. Retrieved June 25, 2021, from https://www.theguardian.com/commentisfree/2014/jul/01/beds-in-sheds-real-victims-housing-crisis-rent

Foucault, M. (1991). Governmentality. In C. Gordon Burchell & P. Miller (Eds.), *The Foucault Effect*. Harvester Wheatsheaf.

Fox, L. (2007). *Conceptualizing Home.* Hart.
Garfinkel, H. (1967). *Studies in Ethnomethodology.*
Hackney Council. (1935). Slum Clearance and Re-Housing by the Council of the Metropolitan Borough of Hackney. Retrieved June 25, 2021, from https://www.londonsscreenarchives.org.uk/title/241/
Hamlin, C. (1998). *Public Health and Social Justice in the Age of Chadwick.* Cambridge University Press.
Hansard. (22 January 2003). Housing (Overcrowding). *HC Deb, 398*, 323–5.
Harvey, O. (2017). Shedsitland: Immigrants Packed in Squalid "£850 a month" Sheds and Garages of West London. *The Sun*, 4 November.
Hunter, R., McGlynn, C., & Rackley, E. (2010). *Feminist Judgments: From Theory to Practice.* Hart.
Jones, R. (2017). Welcome to Rabbit Hutch Britain, Land of the Ever-shrinking Home. *The Guardian*, 11 February.
Kirton-Darling, E. (2018). Safe and Sound: Precariousness, Compartmentation and Death at Home. In H. Carr, B. Edgeworth, & C. Hunter (Eds.), *Law and the Precarious Home: Socio-Legal Perspectives on the Home in Insecure Times.* Hart.
Lacey, N. (2017). Companions on a Serendipitous Journey. *Journal of Law and Society, 44*(2), 283–296.
Leilani, R. (2021). *Luster.* Picador.
Lorey, I. (2015). *State of Insecurity: Government of the Precarious.* Verso.
Manderson, D. (2005). Interstices: New Work on Legal Spaces. *Law, Text Culture, 9.* Retrieved June 25, 2021, from https://ro.uow.edu.au/ltc/vol9/iss1/1
Nelken, D. (2013 [1985]). *The Limits of the Legal Process: A Study of Landlords, Law and Crime.* Kluwer.
Nelken, D. (2020). Beyond Social Constructionism? Cicourel and the Search for Ecoolgical Validity. *Journal of Law and Society, 47*(4), 535–557.
Niemietz, K. (2014). Danny Dorling's "All that is Solid": The Worst Book on the Housing Crisis so far. Retrieved June 25, 2021, from https://iea.org.uk/blog/danny-dorling%E2%80%99s-%E2%80%98all-that-is-solid%E2%80%99-the-worst-book-on-the-housing-crisis-so-far
Notter, J., & Firth, R. (1894). *The Theory and Practice of Hygiene.* Churchill.
O'Donovan, D. (2016). Socio-legal Methodology: Conceptual Underpinnings, Justifications and Practical Pitfalls. In L. Cahillane & J. Schweppe (Eds.), *Legal Research Methods: Principles and Practicalities* (pp. 107–129). Clarus Press.
Osborne, T. (2005). Security and Vitality: Drains, Liberalism and Power in the Nineteenth Century. In A. Barry, T. Osborne, & N. Rose (Eds.), *Foucault and Political Reason* (pp. 99–122). Routledge.
Parkes, E (1866) *A Manual of Practical Hygiene Prepared Especially for Use in the Medial Service of the Army.* Forgotten Books Classic Reprint Series
Polanyi, K. (2001 [1944]). *The Great Transformation: The Political and Economic Origins of Our Time.* Beacon Press.
Ratcliffe, S. (2014). The Condition of England Novel. *British Library*, 15 May. Retrieved June 25, 2021, from https://www.bl.uk/romantics-and-victorians/articles/the-condition-of-england-novel#
Rose, N. (1999). *Powers of Freedom: Reframing Politifcal Thought.* Cambridge University Press.
Rowntree, S. (1901). *Poverty: A Study of Town Life.* Macmillan.

Shelter. (2016). Report: Living Home Standard. Retrieved June 25, 2021, from https://england.shelter.org.uk/professional_resources/policy_and_research/policy_library/report_living_home_standard

Tunstall, R. (2015). Relative Housing Space Inequality in England and Wales, and Its Recent Rapid Resurgence. *International Journal of Housing Policy, 15*(2), 105–126.

Twigg, J. (2002). The Body in Social Policy: Mapping a Territory. *Journal of Social Policy, 31*(3), 421–440.

Twigg, J. (2004). The Body, Gender, and Age: Feminist Insights in Social Gerontology. *Journal of Aging Studies, 18*, 59–73.

Waldron, J. (1991). Homelessness and the Issue of Freedom. *University of California Los Angeles Law Review, 39*, 295.

Wilson, W., & Barton, C. (2020). *Overcrowded Housing (England)*. House of Commons Library Briefing Paper 1013.

Statutes

Housing Act 1935.

Cases

Clark v Manchester City Council [2015] UKUT 0129.

Nottingham City Council v Parr [2018] UKSC 51.

CHAPTER 6

Reading the Body That Was Not Written

Thanos Zartaloudis

Abstract In this chapter, I sketch how I would look for inspiration and sources for the planning and writing of a piece on 'the body and the law', with regard to tracing elements of previous research that could provide a starting point, as well as clarifying some basic parameters that tend to influence my research. The idea posed, ultimately, is that I would explore the notion of the risen body (bodily resurrection) in Paul as a way to reflect on the idea of our species' being as one of metamorphosis. The element of 'law' that I would engage with is largely implied here, but it would be, for the most part, the sense of law in its anthropological element, that of the being of our species, and, for that matter, the absence of such a law.

Keywords Aristotle • Body • Heidegger • Metamorphosis • Paul • Resurrection

Introduction

In the last ten years, my research has focused, for the most part, on theoretical, historical and philosophical inquiries into three different (though sometimes convergent) thematic fields. First, investigating the 'stuff' that 'law', 'right' 'property', 'economy' and so forth are made of (from ancient civilisations to modernity). Second, the movement of peoples and how this has been understood and engaged with in different traditions through time (including

T. Zartaloudis (✉)
University, Canterbury, UK

Center for Hellenic Studies, Harvard University, Washington, DC, USA
e-mail: t.zartaloudis@kent.ac.uk

D. Herman, C. Parsley (eds.), *Interdisciplinarities*, Palgrave Socio-Legal Studies, https://doi.org/10.1007/978-3-030-89297-5_6

religious, legal and futurist traditions). Finally, the planning and design of the built environment with regard to its social-minded uses in terms of architectural, political and legal history and theory (see, e.g. Zartaloudis, 2021). I work 'across disciplines' only in the practical sense of discovering 'on the go' that I may need to engage with material from another field and often at quite a substantial level. Afterall, disciplines are not neat fields but artificial toolboxes; and sometimes the tool you happen to need has been historically misplaced or replaced in another discipline. Inevitably, then, the inspiration for writing a theoretical-historical piece about 'the body and the law' would be drawn from mixed materials and disciplines.

Perhaps it is fitting to note the sense in which I employ the term 'theoretical', rather than risk it being confused with the oft-expressed negative view that theory is self-consumed, detached from reality (note, e.g. that the usual antonym for the word 'theoretical' is said to be the empirical). 'What is theory?', one tends to ask, but this is not a helpful way to think about theory as a practice of thinking and writing. Nor does it help to refer to the occasional synonyms of theory, such as speculation, supposition, conjecture, proposition, hypothesis, conception, explanation, model, and so on in order to shed light on its meaning. Before this kind of definitional question can be raised or rather in order for it to be raised, I tend to approach, at first, almost everything in the manner of cynicism. That most things are quite corrupt would be a cynical and at the same time ironic generalisation, but this sweeping sense can be useful to me since the idea of corruption can then be made particular through an examination. In the ancient sense of the word, corruption can indicate an incomplete and fragmentary construction, rather than some nostalgic sense of past perfection now in ruins. Things are useful because they are irreparably incomplete. There are only ruins. Theoretical ways are really just *ways* in which we can perceive and translate our corrupt experience, our suffering (in the old sense of the word, the *astheneia*), not as a lack but as the affirmation of the absence of a determinate purpose (end or 'nature') for our species. A being that is, among its other qualities, a made-being, something that is constructed and painfully fashioned. Theory, in the sense I employ it here, turns our questioning towards being attentive to practices of conscious and unconscious making/unmaking, so that, when more than less successful, we can make our experience bearable and, verbally as well as non-verbally, communicable.

But let me clarify something further. The earliest attempt to think of the meaning of theory as an activity was, as far as we know, by Aristotle. Aristotle spent, in fact, a long time trying to define the kind of understanding that human beings are capable of, which, to put it in his terms, he called *theoría*. In Aristotle, *theoría* (from the verb *theorein*) comes to mean what we call contemplation, the activity or praxis of reflection (or study) in an at least proximate sense to our modern uses. For example, in *Nicomachean Ethics*, he asks how one can study what is 'good' for human beings? He notices that, unlike the *theoría* of science (*epistēmē*) and of *technē* (the arts), the *theoría* of the good for human beings is essentially a reflective activity that cannot be detached from praxis. While in science or the arts we can disconnect the human factor to an extent and study their objects and artefacts, in ethical theory (or the theory of the good) the 'object' lies *within* the praxis of human contemplation and cannot be separated from it. Aristotle observes that ethical study engages with a *theoría* that is inward-looking without, however, being passive or self-consumed contemplation. *Theoría* is something that is in the very nature of being human, and so Aristotle develops for the first time an understanding of theory that is neither independent of the practical world, nor entirely speculative, in the sense in which perhaps some perceive theory. Theory is a core and crucial part of *how* we are as human beings, given that we cannot know in any definitive sense *what* we are. A human being is an ethical being, by definition, since one does not know in advance what is the good way of life, or what is one's 'essence'. As such a human being experiences its own being in a peculiar manner whereby knowledge or contemplation (*theoría*) cannot be independent to praxis, that is, the very way of existing (one's *ēthos*).

In this understanding, then, theory is the way in which we, as a species, are open to the world, irreparably so and without totality or end. Theory, in this respect, has a much closer sense to what we call the bodily or the living organism, in contrast to the Cartesian scission between body and mind that dominated in modernity. The fantasy of a unified being, ancient or modern, challenges this openness, but in vain since sooner or later only ruins, once more, remain. I would, thus, look at what happens, theoretically and historically, when we say 'the body' in that, for instance, we seem to imply that there is something else that is not 'the body'. This fantasy was, in certain respects, present in the ancient traditions. For example, in Plato's *Alcibiades* I, Socrates says that since the body (*sōma*) cannot rule itself, it must have a ruler, the *psukhē* which he equates with the person (130a1–c6). With this in mind, in order to plan this chapter that I would be writing, I would be asking: is not the term 'body' a term akin to the 'whole' (*sōma*, a Greek word for 'body',[1] had this significance also in the classical and the modern uses of it) or the 'good'? We have thought of the body and embodiment in limited ways, on the basis of the Cartesian body, to determine modes of ordering (think of the old sharp distinctions between the rationality of reason and the irrationality of the senses, etc.) and thus to draw up differences upon which we built identities, constructing particular bodies and relations of normalcy to the world (think of the differentiation between the animal and the human, or the natural and the artifice). I would like to suggest that theory interrogates and constructs, in its manner, the modes of ordering and the modes of making distinctions and producing differences and identities that are particularly difficult to think about in our over-consuming everyday practices. We are autopoietic animals in need of ways of seeing.

The sense of *theoría* or *theorein* as aiming towards this kind of reflective understanding would be key to me in developing a starting point as to writing about the body/organism and law (perhaps the quintessential modes of

[1] On the multiple 'body' terms in Homer, see Vivante, 1955, pp. 39–50.

modern ordering, the *organon* of science and philosophy and the *nomos* of law, its way of attribution, distribution and retribution).[2] Theory, with Aristotle's later key influence, will form the kernel of not only science but also philosophy, mathematics and of what we understand today as theology (observing and speaking of the divine). Before Aristotle, the verb *theorein* meant not so much reflection in the philosophical or ethical sense, but simply to look upon, to observe; and the noun *theoría* meant to look, to look more closely, to observe, to have an experiential insight. As such, theory in its ancient understanding is not affected by the Cartesian distinction between body and mind that we are accustomed to (as well as its classic critiques). Theory, in this sense, was understood as complete in its very exercise: there is no unfolding of a process, no production or development of consequences and no ordinarily practical end point to the practice of theory. Which is another way of saying that 'the body' is synonymous with the *theoretical* practice of making and unmaking human being, and in this sense, theory points towards the immanent ('bodily', if you must) creation of a way of life.

The Personal Is Research

Being invited to think more directly about 'bodily aspects' to law in relation to my work as potentially more significant, than I earlier assumed, would be of interest as it would be an opportunity to focus on the detail of something that interests me. How would I go about trying to conceive of something, at first? The first stage is generally, in my case, a brief state of despair to the point that I very nearly would wish to write to the editors and say that I'd rather not commit to this. The second stage, a day or so later, would be to have a few cups of coffee and browse and read, skim mostly. Then, for some bizarre reason I sleep further on it, and because of a random reference or idea I saw or remembered, or a relevant line that hovers in my mind I would believe in the world of the living anew and consider it possible perhaps to write something. And then, most of the time, I quite manically collect some ideas, threads mostly, loosely, or not at all at first, linked, some readings (often entirely unrelated), some images (of metamorphosis perhaps), some older notes, and after I spent a significant amount of time reading and note-taking, the strange moment of the first sentence comes to mind and once that happens I have usually then written the whole piece in a couple of days. This may also have something to do with having started writing at an early age non-academically as a way to find my world, and, while the later acquired academic writing skills were a valuable addition, they were also a straitjacket that I more or less always resented; especially in law where writing tends to be very dry and doctrinal for the most part, or aims at policy and reform which while I often admire in others, I have little interest in. I think I try, then, to imitate in academic writing the process that I would usually more freely follow in my more personal writing. It may be very

[2] On nomos, see my study Zartaloudis, 2019a.

odd to anyone else, but for me it works and perhaps one transferable aspect of this to your experience of writing may be to experiment with gathering disparate but somehow relevant material, to loosen the imagination and the reasoning that runs through planning a piece, so to find something that genuinely is of interest for you to write about. The reader should be able to locate something of you in your words.

I would, thus, begin by reconsidering formative ideas, in my readings, as to thinking about the body and how the body has surfaced or not in my work this far and explore personal and wider theoretical reasons (such as why do we speak of embodiment?). Along the lines of 'the personal is political' that feminists taught us (a tradition I was immersed in as an undergraduate law student thanks to the many feminist lawyers that taught me at Kent Law School), I find that the personal is equally part of my research and writing in other respects too. This is also another reason why I do not pre-emptively serve a particular set of political or other viewpoints when writing. Stathis Gourgouris describes, in the opening paragraph of his 'Preface' to *The Perils of the One*, an akin sense that feels familiar to me:

> Compositions emerge from some irreducible improvisation, even if they're never actualized and remain just flashes of thought. What enables them to be constituted is a specific time and space that they come to occupy uniquely. This space-time dimension belongs to them fully and may be thought of as the fold within which they are generated. Of course, once actualized, fully composed, and objectified, they belong to the space-time of history, within which they may continue to live or die, freed not only from the author's intentions but from their own parameters of composition. (Gourgouris, 2019)

There is an element to this experience of compositional improvisation that illustrates how one is not in control at a much less abstract level. An aspect that would influence considerably my thinking and planning of a piece on law and the body would derive from my personal experiences with chronic illnesses and how they have transformed and continue to transform the sense of 'my body'. There is a traditional assumption of separation and relational dissonance between 'the body' and 'the mind' on the basis of a traditional Western presupposition of a binarism between matter and spirit, nature and culture, that forms (and deforms, if necessary) the liberal subject. Affirming a scission between 'the body' or 'matter' and the 'ideational' or 'mind', the non-linguistic and the linguistic, is inescapable for our species, but what remains ever open is how to think about it (including in a way other than as a separation that the liberal subject arrives, almost at birth, to miraculously nullify and thus unify). The affirmation of this scission as something that defines our species, necessarily refuses the language of the unified liberal subject, but also of the discourses of materialism and idealism. This is an admittance that I/we are always-already accustomed to *be* in the scission between our non-linguistic and our linguistic body or being, experienced not as a lack but a certain form of passivity, an opening rather than a separation (a trope of thought that is conceived by philosopher Giorgio Agamben).

This experience has indicated to me that there has always been an open mystery in terms of thinking about the notion of the 'body' in my personal reflections. The 'body', to paraphrase Aristotle (who spoke of being), is said in many ways, and thus it has its many ways of communicating; it had its own social media long before social media. The diagnosis of chronic autoimmune diseases since my mid-twenties meant that I have been faced with an arduous process of coming to terms with the thing that is called the 'body.' Autoimmune diseases are conceived by Western medical practice as a 'crisis' when a biological organism essentially attacks 'itself' and compromises its supposed 'integrity'. A body that in a sense says 'no' to itself while the supposed 'self' says no in turn to the body, increasing the turbine of anxiety that leads to a vicious circle of autophagia. This is revealing for the way in which some Western conceptions think of the 'body' in the peculiar sense we have of presuming that there is such a thing as *integrity* in the first place that, if threatened, shatters its-self.

For the vast majority of modern chronic pain sufferers, 'bodily experience assumes enormous proportions' (DelVecchio et al., 1992, p. 37). Patients describe their pain as 'shattering' and 'world-destroying'; and it is of interest to me that in such shattering the thing I had learned to call 'the body' emerged as a symptom of the presupposition of binarism in itself, this 'body' and its integrity emerging as a fragment of fragments, equally shattered along with whatever 'mental' constructions had invented it. Instead, the diseases offered me an opening to what Caroline Bynum has noted poignantly, namely: 'There is no clear set of structures, behaviours, events, objects, experiences, words, and moments to which *body* currently refers' (Bynum, 1995, p. 5). Shattering my presuppositions upon rethinking autoimmunity as not a war between two 'bodies' (e.g. the material and the mental and so forth) unconcealed the binarism that persistently stuttered in front of each autoimmune reaction. Anxiety's inner discourse as a debodied mental state attempts to guard the artifice of the self against listening to the body, it aims to appease self-imposed expectations, but it is indeed not a listening exercise that is needed (for this presupposes a separation still) but one of unlocking the illusion of both the unified or parted self from its shell.

The presupposition of bodily integrity is a fantasy that also misrecognises the body as a unity and often on that basis separates an inside from the outside—for instance, the body in its natural and its cultural capacities, or the body as a self and its environment—founding a sense of antagonistic aspects. Yet, autoimmune diseases, ironically, seem to me to reveal the vacuity of any supposed antagonism (whether between the self and the body or the body and itself). Antagonism presumes a fundamental difference, when there is none. I do consider that there is indeed a gaping gap between our cellular constituencies and the thing we call 'the self' (Cohen, 2004). But, instead of falling into the dominant binary logic of contra-distinction, whereby all that explains the autoimmunity of a disease is a process of the body misrecognising itself as other than itself (as a disease), the hypersensitive reaction of the immune system seems to me to indicate instead our organism as a dynamic opening, rather than a frontier crossed by a self-hating body/self (see Varela, 1991). 'Life is a window of vulnerability', as Donna Haraway puts it (1991, p. 224), and vulnerability reveals a contingent being without ends, which is another way to say: without integrity. This has meant that thinking about the body emerges for me out of an affirmative fragmentation, necessitating a continuous sense of reconstruction, and so I would start thinking about what to write with this very sense of the loss of an integral point that, instead, is the place of a continuous multiplier of possibilities.

The Body Is 'the Most Difficult Problem'

I have been generally influenced by reading Martin Heidegger's works over the past 20 years. It was particularly striking when reading Heidegger to note his admission in his *Heraclitus Seminars* of 1966–1967 that the body is 'the most difficult problem' (Heidegger & Fink, 1979, p. 147).[3] Some things are marked in our memory, and this was one of those moments that stayed with me. I admired the admission in itself—it is not frequent that a thinker admits a limitation. I got the impression of a marking, a limit, something that really needed to be thought, despite the declared difficulty. Thus, I would be revisiting this while trying to conceive of the piece I would write. 'What is at stake here for me?' is the question I often ask when trying to write something. As it happens, Heidegger is often misread, I find, as if his admission indicated neglect of the body or some kind of a polemic. There are specific reasons why Heidegger made this admission, not just as a matter of drawing a limit, but as an encounter with a limit. A few years after the *Heraclitus Seminars*, towards the very end of the famous *Zollikon*, decade-long, seminars where the bodily is ever more engaged with, he writes: 'the bodily [*das Leibliche*] is the most difficult [problem to understand] and I was unable to say more at the time' (Heidegger, 2001, p. 231). It is misleading to suggest neglect, here, because, if one reads Heidegger, one finds so many instances where he encounters the bodily and engages with it, that it would be strange to miss all these moments in his work and conclude otherwise.

In his earliest work, on Aristotle, Heidegger wrote some of the most remarkable pages on the problem of facticity and mood (Heidegger, 1988a). In his major early work *Being and Time* (1962 [1927]), he examines the spatial directionality of the body in particular. In his 1936–1937 Nietzsche Lectures (Heidegger, 1991) and in the 1946/1947 'Letter on Humanism' (Heidegger, 1977 [1947]), among other writings, even more so. In fact, I was startled when I read in *Being and Time* (Division 1, Chapter 6) that one is always-already in a mood (*Stimmung*) and that this is to be understood as one of the

[3] Also noted earlier: '*Dasein's* bodily nature hides a whole problematic of its own' in Heidegger, 1962, p. 143.

most essential ways of disclosing human existence. I remember noting down humorously 'no orientation without anxiety' and that the question is not 'are you anxious?', but 'are you anxious enough?' In a way, detachment (anxiety) as the key mode of *engagement* in philosophy was something that not only touched a personal chord, but in its paradoxicity drew me in further. Yet, this is not the place to go into the detail of all this. I am just noting this because of the specific influence that it has had in my own thinking and the fact that it would influence my way towards writing something on the body.

More importantly, it is of particular relevance that Heidegger does not engage with the old, but fundamental for the Western tradition, Cartesian polarity of the body as bounded, as a material substance extended in space, a body that can be scientifically observed, be handled as corporeal and so on. He aims to overcome this from the start by speaking of a lived-body (*Leib*). A body that has lived, living, is not something that I encounter as a means, or a container, or indeed as something that is foreign, mute, but instead as something that is 'always-already' (*immer schon*) involved; the body is an essential existentiale (*Existenzial*) condition of being (*Dasein, being-the-there*; Heidegger's term to avoid using the terms 'subject', 'human' etc.) (see Haugeland, 1992; Cerbone, 2000; Frede & Reis, 2009). This is also the reason why Heidegger does not offer a theory of the body as something that could be separated as an object, even as an object of study. The philosophical reason for not doing so is actually due to the very attempt of using this new term *Dasein*, to reflect on everyday human existence and embodied lived-being, as something that precedes the emergence of the notion of the human body. Heidegger in his seminars in Zollikon writes, thirty years after *Being and Time*:

> The *Da* in *Being and Time* does not mean a statement of place for a being, but rather it should designate the open-ness where beings can be present for the human being, and the human being also for himself. The *Da* of [*Dasein's*] being distinguishes the humanness of the human being. (Heidegger, 2001, p. 120)

As it happens, this formed the main line of inquiry in my doctoral thesis. Hence, both the corporeal body (as an object) and the lived body (as a subject) are critiqued for failing to mark what is more crucial in understanding our existence as *Dasein*. This is often misunderstood as suggesting that we need to precede any inquiry into the bodily with some general, abstract theory of being. Yet, Heidegger's point here is not as to originality, in the sense of prehistorically, hierarchically and metaphysically, but instead in the sense of experience (experience and how to think of what we call 'experience' is in a sense synonymous to the problem of the body, and this may be in fact why it is the *hardest* problem). It is worth noting also that experience later on becomes near synonymous to *theorein* in the sense of observation and also experimentation. Linked to the Greek ἐμπειρίᾱ (*empeiriā*) and possibly linked to the Ionic Greek form of πέρας (*peras*), 'end, limit, boundary', experience could be thought, quite fittingly, as attempting to cross a limit.

How is one to think of the bodily, if one finds problematic the naturalistic, subjectifying and objectifying sense of bodies as an internal-outside, the idea that one 'has' a body, or, equally, that there is such a thing as a 'mere' natural or biological body? (Heidegger, 1991, in particular, vol. 1, pp. 99–100). We, as *dasein*, as *ex*-istent, Heidegger teaches, are already in a world, which paradoxically means that we 'are' already stepped out, beyond 'ourselves' (*ex-sistere*) (Heidegger, 1988b). As a species, we have a dynamic way of being, in that, while we are conditioned by our planetary existence in various ways, like other animals, we are also conditioned by existing within cultural meaning, and as such we are neither bounded nor isolated by the avatars of skin, or kin. Our stories of ourselves and our bodies are always skewed (Plato, *Timaeus*, 34b10–35a1).

Where Would I Start?

Thinking and writing about the body, whether in relation to law or not, has not been central to my work, in the sense that I have never written anything directly addressing 'the body' or the significant scholarship that relates to it. In more recent years, however, I have had some aspects of the bodily emerge in my work. Being invited to write specifically on law and the body, I would be engaging with more or less, then, a new angle to my interests, but I would probably do so by revisiting my earlier published research and notebooks in order to find a thread I can relate to. For example, in my last monograph *The Birth of Nomos* (2019a), where I studied, among else, archaic epic and other literature in order to find clues for the uses of *nomos*, a term that eventually somehow became associated centuries later with a certain notion of law, the body surfaced only occasionally. Nomos (from the verb *nemein*) is, for example, associated with a certain sense of distribution, and it is used in some instances to describe the spread of a disease, or the movement of the legs when walking. To give you a better sense of the more particular way in which I would trace the bodily in my earlier work in order to find something interesting to investigate, it is probably useful to give you a better sense of another of my subsequent engagements with the bodily that I think I would be keen to further.

In research I did more recently, I studied the extant original sources that describe the practices of ancient Greek supplication (petitioning), and I engaged with bodily aspects more directly for the first time (see Zartaloudis, 2019b). The use of the body was described in terms of ritualised gestures that effected a prayer or as some have it a 'process', speculating that one sees this as a comparable (though indirect) ancient precursor to what we schematically understand by asylum (while such supplicatory practices are not to be confused with the later ancient Greek *asylia*). This led me to consider what is the effect of thinking 'with' archaic physical gestures on what is called in a modern sense 'the body' (Bremmer, 1991, pp. 23–26). This is particularly interesting when it comes to supplication given that the first indication of an act of supplication is usually the adoption of a particular bodily posture (see Gernet, 1968, pp. 229–233). Posture is not, however, a mere 'physical' attribute for the Greeks. In a sense, a particular posture is the initial element of the rite of supplication in the archaic period (and beyond), and it is certainly a non-binary gesture that forms one of the most important non-linguistic signs of supplication as a threshold-crossing (see Giordano, 1999, pp. 21ff; and Lateiner, 1995, pp. 93–103). The *hiketēs* prostrates himself/herself at, for example, the knees of the benefactor, launches towards him/her lowering his/her stature, curling up, crouching down indicating debasement but also a chthonic state of near-death (Haugeland, 1992). The assimilation to the one supplicating to the earth is not a minor detail. Rather it is a key to the understanding of the gesture of supplication in its relation to the chthonic (divine) earth (ibid., p. 21). Mortal existence is a vector of cosmic powers, so that the bodily gestures of the suppliant are an appeal to (and in contact with) the forces of the earth (see Gould, 1973, p. 95). Thus, the potential threat of contamination (pollution, *miasma*) emanating from maltreating or ignoring such pleas was something that was felt to a terrifying degree (Gernet, 1968, pp. 229–233).[4]

This led me to think, and it is this thread that I would pursue in the piece I would write, of a supplicatory 'bodily' gesture as a threshold-experience whereby the suppliant's posture indicates marginalisation and even a negation of 'individuality', a 'coming to' or 'from' another sphere, a being 'without qualities', a *becoming*-stranger. The archaic sense of 'the body' is notably interesting to study not because it can teach us something that is similar/useful to what we understand today as to the body, but rather *because* it is very different. In the archaic Greek, *sōma* is neither understood through some kind of 'binary structure' of *sōma and psuchē* (body and soul), nor was there a term to designate the 'body' as, say, an 'organic unity' (Ceyte, 2003, p. 49f; see also Vernant, 1991). It was revealing, in fact, that *sōma* and *psuchē* in the Homeric epic refer not to the sphere of the living but of the dead. The corpse of an enemy in the Iliadic battlefield deprived of proper funerary rites cannot continue to 'exist' in the sphere of the mortals, and so this abandoned body is referred to as *sōma* (and that applies to animal bodies also).[5] The 'materiality of the body' as one would say today, is a shapeless body, bare, and as such a terrifying experience for the Greeks. In a way, this confirmed my hypothesis that there is no self-evident 'body' (or 'matter') and that instead in order to explore the specific ways in which *sōma* is used in the archaic and classical periods (until it is in one sense conceptualised through early medical treatises), one needs to dissociate from anachronistic senses of the body.

The notion of supplication as a threshold experience unexpectedly, a year or so later, became connected in my thinking in research that I was doing which focused on the experience of migration in the trope of a metamorphosis (see Zartaloudis, 2021). As a migrant, I found myself asking the question of whether the experience of moving to another place is not, in one sense, akin to that of

[4] For the myth of Carila in relation to this, see Plutarch *Quaestiones Graecae* 293d.1–293f.5.
[5] See, for example, Homer, *Iliad* 3.22; 18.161; and *Odyssey* 11.51–53; 12.67.

a threshold-experience, the seeking of another chance (obviously in a varied sense and intensity among migrants). I was since childhood, through reading Arabic literature and Russian fairy tales in particular, captivated and curious about the experience of metamorphosis, and in my adult life I have been thinking, occasionally, of why metamorphosis has been so prevalent in literature from ancient times till today. Metamorphosis could be thought of in the sense that our species, lacking an essence, constantly metamorphosises in a love-hate relation with the legal-political-economic forms and processes that morph us into citizens and denizens and which are trying to halt this continuous transformation for logistical and politico-economic reasons. As I am currently thinking a lot about metamorphosis as our species' normalcy in relation to what we call 'nature' (in a new project on the ancient uses of the term *physis* in relation to modern theories of autopoiesis), I would probably find the invitation to think about law and the body as an opportunity to follow this speculative lead in conjunction with my earlier work on supplication as a threshold experience and see where it takes me.

Resurrection: Researching the Body Without Ends

Having had an interest in the Christian traditions and theology (Western and Eastern) and a longer-term research aim to study early Christianity, I have had in mind for some years now to explore Paul in particular, so I would probably find this invitation a good opportunity to take another step towards this aim by examining the way in which resurrection is described in Paul. In my notebooks I have been gathering evidence of notions of bodily resurrection in Greek and Roman literary evidence, magical and religious practices (see, e.g. Odgen, 2001). I would probably start there in order to appreciate the context of the traditions within which early Christianity and Paul convey earlier traditions and develop their ideas further. In addition, having been researching magical practices in ancient traditions, I noticed the many different ways in which necromancy (and in a sense resurrection) was practised in the extant evidence of the Magical Papyri (see Preisendanz & Henrichs, 1973–1974; and Dieter, 1986). I would be keen to note and study further the way in which the resurrection of the dead is a core belief in all the Abrahamic religions and, perhaps, having read Maimonides in the past, I would on this occasion re-engage with the importance of the belief in rabbinic Judaism.

Furthermore, I would probably need to re-examine relevant elements in Plato and Aristotle given the influence that they had in Christian theology and in particular in the three key medieval Aristotelians: Thomas Aquinas, John Duns Scotus and William Ockham who all had a great interest in thinking about bodily resurrection (*resurrectio carnis* or *mortuorum*). There would be a lot of material from which to select what to focus on, but on such a vast topic this difficulty is in fact a blessing (see, indicatively, Cornelis et al., 1964; Nickelsburg 1972; Crouzel & Grossi, 1992). What would eventually make it into the piece would probably be a minuscule part of the notes, but learning to economise when writing a piece is a skill you can nurture if your notes are significantly larger than anything you publish. In order to ascertain some starting points in such wealth among different traditions, I would, normally, focus on asking what seem like general and basic questions that could guide my searches. Yet more often than not in my experience, the most important question is also the simplest: why did early Christians, for example, passionately and at great length attempt to formulate and argue for bodily resurrection? What was at stake?

The notion of the body as a natural body or a spiritual body is already preeminent in one of the earliest Christian texts (I *Cor* 15), but 'in what way?' is the key question I would explore. Many significant and lengthy controversies and debates, such as Gnosticism, Docetism, Origenism and so forth, were essentially battles fought over these images of resurrection. My working hypothesis would be that these matters ultimately centred directly or indirectly on the notion of divine power (*potentia*, *dynamis*), a notion that I have worked on before in the ancient Greek and medieval theological, legal and philosophical context. This I would aim to bring to closer inspection with regard to the different ways in which the body is conceived (*sōma* or *corpus*, *sarx* or *caro*), as a genealogy of the political theology of the body (whether in terms of imaginative and merely metaphorical uses of resurrection or in spiritualist attempts to escape the body, nature and this world). It would in fact probably point me anew to the long story of how materialism prevailed in the West since the twelfth century and how this has had repercussions to this very day. I would also be keen to ask how this has informed the traditions of law in the west, as well as the Pauline conception of eschatological somatology whereby a particular notion of the *sōma* forms a core element of Pauline ideas of fulfilling the 'law'. I have a preliminary sense that the transformation of the risen body in Paul (e.g. in *Rom* 8.23 and *Phil* 3.21) forms an eschatology of what I call present futures, so I would be keen to examine if that line of thought can feed on the original texts.

But before I could explore the possible connection to lines of thought I have pursued earlier in terms of a threshold experience or metamorphosis, I would have to first explore some key and more specific methodological issues. For instance, it is not clear what resurrection is in Paul even at the literary level. I would probably start by a philological and contextual analysis of the Pauline texts. Within this philological approach, I would need to study the main strands of interpretation as to the literal and metaphorical senses of the risen body. Given that I was occupied by the metaphorical in my earlier piece on metamorphosis in relation to the experience of migration, this would probably point me to a similar problem as to what metaphor does to a discourse of resurrection. The literal interpretation would appear to me to stress too much the reality of the fiction, missing the point that fiction is real in itself. Pitting the two discourses of metaphoricity and literality against each other, as is often the case, would potentially exhaust the energies of interpretation without much resolution, since it would, in one shade or another, insist on the separation of cognition and physical reality. One does not observe or have a *sōma*, one is *sōma*. Yet, this does not mean that one's *sōma* is a unified experience of existence. Hence, my key question in this, preliminary, piece would be something along the lines of one aspect of the whole that would give me a way in but also indicate the next steps: what is the meaning and what is at stake in the Pauline expression *σῶμα πνευματικόν* (*sōma pneumatikon*; 1 *Cor* 15: 44), if we push aside the artificial and largely anachronistic separation between *sōma* (as body) and *pneuma* (as spirit)?

References

Bremmer, J. (1991). Walking, Standing and Sitting in Ancient Greek Culture. In J. Bremmer & H. Rodenburg (Eds.), *A Cultural History of Gesture from Antiquity to the Present Day*. Cambridge University Press.

Bynum, C. (1995). Why All This Fuss About the Body? A Medievalists' Perspective. *Critical Inquiry, 22*(1), 1–33.

Cerbone, D. R. (2000). Heidegger and Dasein's "Bodily Nature": What Is the Hidden Problematic? *International Journal of Philosophical Studies, 8*(2), 209–230.

Ceyte, J. (2003/1). La corporéité en Grèce archaïque. Un réseau socio-cosmique. *Hypothèses, 6*, 49–58.

Cohen, E. (2004). My Self as an Other: On Autoimmunity and "Other" Paradoxes. *Medical Humanities, 30*, 7–11.

Cornelis, H., Guillet, J., Camelot, T., & Genevois, M. A. (1964). *The Resurrection of the Body, Themes of Theology*. Fides.

Crouzel, H., & Grossi, V. (1992). Resurrection of the Dead. In A. Di Berardino (Ed.), *Encyclopaedia of the Early Church* (2 vols., A. Walford, Trans.). Oxford University Press.

DelVecchio Good, M.-J., Brodwin, P. E., Good, B. J., Kleinman, A., & Hilbert, R. A. (1992). *Pain as Human Experience: An Anthropological Perspective* (p. 37). University of California Press.

Dieter, H. (Ed.). (1986). *The Greek Magical Papyri in Translation*. University of Chicago Press.

Frede, D., & Reis, B. (Eds.). (2009). *Body and Soul in Ancient Philosophy*. Walter de Gruyter.

Gernet, L. (1968). *Anthropologie de la Grèce antique*. F Maspéro.

Giordano, M. (1999). *La supplica. Rituale, istituzione sociale e tema épico in Omero*. Istituto universitario orientale.

Gould, J. (1973). Hiketeia. *Journal of Hellenic Studies, 93*, 74–103.

Gourgouris, S. (2019). *The Perils of the One*. Columbia University Press.

Haraway, D. (1991). *The Biopolitics of Postmodern Bodies: Constitutions of Self in Immune Discourse. Simians, Cyborgs, and Women: The Reinvention of Nature*. Routledge.

Haugeland, J. (1992). Dasein's Disclosedness. In H. L. Dreyfus & H. Hall (Eds.), *Heidegger: A Critical Reader*. Blackwell.

Heidegger, M. (1962 [1927]). *Being and Time* (J. Macquarrie & E. Robinson, Trans.). Harper & Row.

Heidegger, M. (1977 [1947]). *Martin Heidegger, Basic Writings* (D. Farrell Krell, Ed.). Harper & Row. pp. 190–242.
Heidegger, M. (1988a). *Ontologie (Hermeneutik der Faktizität)* (vol. 63, K. Bröcker-Oltmanns, Ed.), Gesamtausgabe, Klostermann; published in English as (1999) *Ontology: The Hermeneutics of Facticity* (J. van Buren, Trans.). Indiana University Press.
Heidegger, M. (1988b). *The Basic Problems of Phenomenology* (Rev. ed., A. Hofstadter, Trans.). Indiana University Press.
Heidegger, M. (1991). *Nietzsche* (vols. 1, 2, 3 and 4, D. Farrell Krell, Trans.). HarperOne.
Heidegger, M. (2001). *Zollikon Seminars: Protocols—Conversations—Letters* (M. Boss, Ed., and F. K. Mayr & R. Askay, Trans.). Northwestern University Press.
Heidegger, M., & Fink, E. (1979). *Heraclitus Seminar 1966–67* (T. N. Charles & H. Seibart, Trans.). University of Alabama Press.
Lateiner, D. (1995). *Sardonic Smile, Nonverbal Behavior in Homeric Epic*. University of Michigan Press.
Nickelsburg Jr, G. W. E. (1972). Resurrection, Immortality and Eternal Life in Intertestamental Judaism. *Harvard Theological Studies 26*, Harvard University Press.
Odgen, D. (2001). *Greek and Roman Necromancy*. Princeton University Press.
Preisendanz, K., & Henrichs, A. (Eds.). (1973–1974). *Papyri Graecae Magicae Die Griechischen Zauberpapyri* (vols. I–II). Teubner.
Varela, F. (1991). Organism: A Meshwork of Selfless Selves. In A. Tauber (Ed.), *Organism and the Origins of Self*. Kluwer Academic Publishers.
Vernant, J.-P. (1991). Mortals and Immortals: The Divine Body. In J.-P. Vernant & F. I. Zeitlin (Eds.), *Mortals and Immortals: Collected Essays* (pp. 27–49). Princeton University Press.
Vivante, P. (1955). Sulla Designazione del Corpo in Omero. *Archivio Glottologico Italiano*. Firenze.
Zartaloudis, T. (2019a). *The Birth of Nomos*. Edinburgh University Press.
Zartaloudis, T. (2019b). Hieros Anthropos—An Inquiry into the Practices of Archaic Greek Supplication. *Law and Humanities, 13*(1), 52–75.
Zartaloudis, T. (2020). The Experience of Migration: From Metaphor to Metamorphosis. *On_Culture*, Special Issue on Migration as Metaphor (December 2020–Spring 2021).
Zartaloudis, T. (2021). Lines of Architectural Potency. *AR/Architecture Research Journal*, Special 2020 Issue on The Line: Notes on Politics.

CHAPTER 7

Working with an Example of the Body: Legal Thinking as Method in Interdisciplinary Cultural Studies

Connal Parsley

Abstract In this account of a hypothetical book chapter on 'the body', I describe how I would devise a chapter using the technique of writing through a single example—particularly, a single representation of the body. The chapter discusses some methodological aspects of this choice of method, as well as its appropriateness to the theme of 'the body' in relation to law. It addresses practical concerns like selecting an example, and the 'enabling constraint' the method offers to the writing process. Working with a single example is presented as a matter of bringing disparate materials into a 'constellation' in order to make the example 'more itself', by exploring the conditions and patterns that it makes uniquely visible. The aim of this approach would be to bring together interrelated reflections on how bodies are made meaningful through representational techniques in concrete instances and for specific purposes; the political ontology of representationalism in relation to legal thinking and methods; and scholarly work as an active, critical participant in the acculturation of techniques and ontologies, via the reflexive repurposing of elements of legal thinking.

I would like to thank Didi Herman, Maria Drakopoulou and Shaun McVeigh for comments on a draft version. Errors, omissions and lines left unpursued are all mine.

C. Parsley (✉)
Kent Law School, University of Kent, Canterbury, UK
e-mail: c.parsley@kent.ac.uk

D. Herman, C. Parsley (eds.), *Interdisciplinarities*, Palgrave Socio-Legal Studies, https://doi.org/10.1007/978-3-030-89297-5_7

Keywords Humanities methodologies • Legal techniques • Representation • Political ontology • Exemplarity • Constellation

Introduction

Despite being influenced by disciplines, writers and individual pieces of writing for whom it is a central concern, I have never directly addressed the body in my writing. Wondering why, I look through some of my past work. The body has often been just a breath away from subjects I have considered closely (images of torture, thumbprint evidence in Australia's stolen generations litigation, asylum-seeker processing). Many of the thinkers I draw upon problematise the body or biology (mainly from biopolitical and political theological perspectives). I have also addressed the body directly in my teaching. Two images come to mind—a waxy-looking ear grafted into the skin of a white forearm; naked, starkly-lit bodies suspended by piercing hooks—from the work of Melbourne-based artist Stelarc, who also holds an honorary PhD in law. I've been showing these images in a lecture on transgressive art for an undergraduate module at Kent Law School, 'Art, Law and Politics'. For some years, I was part of a guest teaching team on a multidisciplinary course about the body, at the now-defunct Centre for Ideas at the Victorian College of the Arts in Melbourne (Stelarc was too, or so I gleaned from the lecture schedule). I used to give a lecture on 'Law and the Body', which presented two main critical jurisprudential ideas: that legal discourse depends on the entwining of biological and symbolic life while keeping them rhetorically separated; and that legal aesthetics normatively acculturate a certain *kind* of body. Looking over the lecture again, I wonder if I should write it up for the edited collection. But it seems too diffuse; panoramic and general, and pitched at the wrong audience.

Perhaps some part of it could be expanded? The lecture proceeded in three phases. The first set the stage by arguing that 'law needs a body'. I began with the doctrine of *habeas corpus.* This principle leverages the body and its appearance before the court as a mechanism against unlawful detention, but also makes freedom subject to the power of arrest and the jurisdiction of the court. In a second sense, 'the law needs a body' in that its claim to coherence and authority has often been linked to its presentation as a single 'body'; most famously in Justinian's *Corpus Juris Civilis.* For a contemporary Australian sensibility, more compelling is Peter Rush's nuanced reading of the decision in *Mabo (No 2)*, 'An Altered Jurisdiction: Corporeal Traces of Law'. I'm still impressed by Rush's argument that foundational anxiety about Australian common law's ability to represent 'itself and its other' leads to a specific 'mode' and 'affective economy of representation' (Rush, 1997, p. 149). Rush points to then Chief Justice Brennan's figuration of the 'skeleton of principle' in the 'body of our law' which has 'shape and internal consistency', having 'organic[ally] develop[ed] from' the law of England, and which should not be 'fractured'.[1]

Though this makes me nostalgic for the attentive critical jurisprudence I associate with a treasured PhD supervisor, I don't see anything I could 'make my own'. The other parts of the lecture don't fare much better. The second catalogued some of the ways that 'law controls bodies'. This obvious point served mainly as a conceptual stepping-stone to the more interesting third part on how 'law produces bodies', drawing on ideas I thought would resonate with creative arts students: Foucauldian disciplinary power, 'somatechnic' understandings of bodies as products of historical and cultural discursive practices, and law as an authoritative 'poiesis'. I concluded by exploring the aesthetic dimension of this production, which I allusively (i.e. weakly) presented as a consequence of the normative texture of the juridical imaginary. My main example was the well-known case of *R v Brown*,[2] where the court held that some kinds of (sadomasochistic) acts between men can't be consented to—thus tracing a constrictive imaginary silhouette for the lawful (homosexual) body.

I doubt I'd be able to do anything very original or worthwhile with any of this. Something also sits uneasily about confronting 'the body' directly. It's so overloaded, and has been the centre of so many feminist critical enquires, including in legal scholarship, that I risk ignorantly reinventing various wheels. An oblique strategy starts to form, sparked by Rush's connection between the legal self-imaginary and the legal economy of representation. This resonates with a major focus of my work over the past ten or so years, which has re-read Giorgio Agamben's thought in order to critically address connections between political ontologies of representationalism, law and legal scholarly epistemology. I argue that the significance of Agamben's work lies less in its historical or political accounts of law and legal power, and more in modelling post-representational epistemologies through the Western canon; my aim is to identify a potential resource for the reconceptualisation of jurisprudential thinking. I am currently concluding this work, and drawing it into a more applied project on law, technology and the notion of the 'human'. But I have also been developing its key ideas as part of an ongoing collaboration with some colleagues, on law and humanities methods and methodology. I conclude that publishing a piece bringing some of these concerns together in a demonstrated 'reading' of an instance, image or 'representation' of a body might usefully extend my existing work into more methodological terrain.

Given this motivation, I would decide to focus narrowly on a single example. This would let 'reading' techniques and the notion of a 'legal poietic somatechnics' occupy the foreground, while downplaying substantive claims, the spectre of quantitative issues or 'social effects', and undue theoretical 'knife sharpening'. I have often developed my publications in just this way, by

[1] *Mabo v Queensland (No 2)* (1992) 175 CLR 1, 28, Brennan CJ.
[2] [1993] 2 All ER 75.

thinking through a single object or instance that I think is of unusual cultural-legal significance and tells a broader but perhaps concealed story about the cultural-political life of law. Even where I have 'started with practices' in Foucault's sense, I have tended to make questions of representation, spectacle, and staging central. Though this became more and more deliberate, until now I have just as deliberately avoided theoretical or methodological 'apologias' for this strategy. I have believed that my analyses are more effective when they present, position and analyse examples the way legal discourses try to: as 'natural' or 'self-evident', while in fact supporting particular narratives or imaginaries, without highlighting the hermeneutic frameworks that might reveal their contingency and so render them contestable.[3]

My hypothetical book chapter would thus provide me with an opportunity to reflect more explicitly on the role, nature and use of 'the example' in law, legal thinking and scholarship, and to address the acculturation of a particular political ontology—a particular condition of how things can 'be' politically—by considering a single example of the body and its representation or appearance. In this sense, it would be an attempt to both write *about* legal thinking and to take up one of its technical strategies in order to explore its alternative uses—a kind of *use* of legal thinking as a method for critical scholarship. By considering these technical and methodological questions, I would hope to reflect on the way legal scholarship participates in the production of influential knowledge about law, in turn reflexively considering the place I occupy as a legal scholar in historical and cultural context.

In the next section of this chapter, I explore some pragmatic dimensions of this choice to write through one example. In the section entitled 'Background Preparation: Situating a Method Methodologically', I discuss some of the background work that would go into deepening my knowledge of that choice as a matter of the relationship between method and methodology, before turning, in the section on 'Exemplarity Studies, Not-theory and Knowing the Example', to how I would situate my hypothetical chapter within studies of exemplarity. In pursuing this strategy, a lot hinges on what specific example I choose, which will be the analysis' central enabling—and limiting—factor. In the penultimate section, I discuss example selection, before turning in the last section to consider the pressures and exigencies involved in writing up this chapter on the body in relation to law.

Why Work Through One Example?

There are several practical benefits to working through one example. These benefits are particularly clear for what is often thought of as 'theoretical work', especially when working in an area new or tangential to the author, who might lack confidence in their knowledge of related literatures. First, selecting a

[3] This idea has been widely addressed in critical legal studies. See Young, 1998; re: images, see, for example, Sherwin, 2012, see also Manderson, 2015.

contemporary example can underwrite the originality of a piece of writing, while narrowing the range of literatures to consider by introducing concrete criteria of relevance. My first publication, on the interview process for 'unauthorised arrivals' at Australian airports prior to the moment of legal decision-making, centred on a copy of the process flow chart that I was able to obtain from an immigration department employee (Parsley, 2003). I used this central object to connect material bureaucratic practices to the ethical deficit of governmental decisions, within a Derridean and postcolonial framework. Adding little to Derrida studies or the ethics of decision-making, this piece still made a contribution at the level of border and immigration studies in the Australian context. Second, guided by the old writerly adage 'show don't tell', working through an example can result in a more strongly grounded analysis since it means always having to check that the example supports the author's claims. And by renouncing a more expansive or abstract frame—ensuring that the analysis neither exceeds its support nor 'floats in a text too big for it'[4]—both writer and reader experience greater confidence in the argument's solidity, being equipped with a clear means to test and contest it. This, of course, has a flip side, in that the example will seriously limit the parameters of the analysis. Third, the exigencies of the example can be helpful for the task of settling on a structure, which can be a vertiginous prospect for conceptual work. The concrete example must be introduced and key dimensions unpacked, which gets the ball rolling and removes at least some variables. Depending on the example, when unpacked further it can often do further heavy lifting for the writer: consideration of its details, origins, enigmas, internal structure, or reception in existing literature can generate categories through which to organise an analysis or identify what needs the most careful thought and explanation. Finally, especially if the central example is not a strictly legal one, it can operate as a kind of 'lingua franca' that cuts across different disciplines handling the same 'object' in different ways. This is similar to the effect of taking seriously a particular key concept, theoretical framework, or the proper name of a scholar whose work is itself a topic of study—all things that unite disparate scholarly communities in the humanities and social sciences. These broader communities can be useful in condensing difficult literatures, overviewing conceptual structures, or contextualising them within intellectual traditions. Equally, these literatures can throw into relief the specific concerns and questions of critical legal thinking. If handled carefully, other scholarly communities can become important interlocutors. Sometimes, concealed affinities can emerge that may be more meaningful than those within one's own discipline.

[4] As Jean Baudrillard memorably said of Michel Foucault's writing (Baudrillard, 2007, p. 29).

Background Preparation: Situating a Method Methodologically

These pragmatic factors only go so far, however. For the hypothetical book chapter, I would want to explore the methodological and epistemological conditions of working through a single example, hoping to deepen my understanding of my own disciplinary object, ethos and strategy of critical scholarship. I have a hunch that the 'body chapter' would let me do that by considering how this form and genre relate to substantive claims about technical legal practices of representation. I would be trying to find an angle that could be brought into the overt discussion in the text, so that methodological concerns and knowledge claims are quilted into substantive ones. I would be trying to learn more about how legal epistemologies work with the body, and how the body and its meaning are 'vulnerable' to techniques of representation and appearance. I would anticipate being able to connect legal strategies of representation of the body to broader political ontologies, for example, nature-artifice distinctions that are central in law, or, depending on the example I end up with, understandings of the body in contemporary culture.

Whereas I said above that I have preferred to leave these methodological or epistemological choices 'untheorised' or unarticulated in my work, this piece would require me to make them central. To prepare, my first step would be some preliminary broader reflection on the question of which traditions and disciplines use the technique of working through a single example. What various purposes does it serve, what kinds of techniques does it underpin, and what kinds of knowledge claims does it enable? This will be important in forming, and not only situating, my impressions about the nature of legal representation techniques and the specific agency and responsibility of legal scholarship. A principal way that I learn about legal thinking is by comparing its operations and patterns to other kinds of thought. I find that this generates comparative, situated insights that may not come from reading legal materials and commentary. As a legal scholar drawing on broader intellectual disciplines and traditions, I also try to imagine how my work might be legible to scholars from those fields: for example, which of their concepts, debates or central oppositions might help me to identify and frame issues, and in turn become specific points of contact between disciplines.

In this case, I would look for writing on the status of examples in two main disciplines. First, cultural anthropology (as well as media studies and visual anthropology). These fields were forged through controversies in epistemology and battles over methodology, which are often still described as clashes between 'objective' and 'subjective' anthropology, or the influence of either the 'hard' sciences or the humanities. Versions of similar debates, transduced through structuralism, systems theory and particularly post-structuralism, still generate highly influential work on empiricism, scholarly method, epistemology and ontology in the production of social reality (Law, 2004). Recent studies take positions that seem directly relevant to my methodological assumptions, for example, by prioritising the subject-viewer's embeddedness or participation (a major theme at least since Malinowski's qualitative ethnography), and the adoption of anti-representational understandings of the subject-object relation, which I also emphasise in my work (Kohn, 2013; Viveiros de Castro, 2014). The second discipline that I would explore further, in some ways in tension with the first, is art history. This diverse field has taken radically contrasting aims and orientations,[5] but one of its central tensions is between the specificity of individual works of art, on the one hand, and a range of 'historical' dimensions, on the other (e.g. conceptual, cultural, aesthetic, structural, political-economic), especially understood as the 'defining contours of a distinct period' (Julius, 2003, 'Preface'). Here too, recent influential work helpfully takes up the impulse to treat artworks as individually as possible as a methodological principle of intrinsic significance for the understanding of contemporary art and, by extension, 'the contemporary' as a historical denotation (Groys, 2016).

Reflecting on these fields may shape the claims and overall argument I end up making about a specific representation of the body, even if I'm unlikely to address them directly in my text. I would not pastiche these disciplines by claiming to work within or even with them. Yet, neither would my focus be entirely on what Annelise Riles calls the 'agency of technocratic legal form' (Riles, 2005). The kinds of 'forms' in issue, as epistemological practices, span 'formal' and 'informal' techniques and are necessarily distributed across sites of culture and knowledge production. It may not make sense to understand them as 'legal' (unless the example mandates it). So what I would be interested in through exploring these other disciplines is how the changing 'ends' of their intellectual practices—their variously stated 'purposes'—relate to their knowledge claims, methods and treatment of the individual example, and how legal techniques, legal scholarship and my own handling of my chosen 'example' might compare. The volume's theme of the body helps here, since both of the above fields have also handled 'the body' as a central concern,[6] and I might find interesting parallels or contrasts in how bodies are 'known' in these fields. More generally, I would look for parallel historical controversies around the relationship between fields of practice, scholarly analysis, and the possibility or discoverability of universals and 'laws' (once a common aim). Finally, it's helpful to see how the shifts in these discourses map against the history of changing epistemological qualities of legal thought and practice, which has its own history of flux under the influence of the sciences and social sciences (see Sugarman, 1992; Constable, 1994; Murphy, 1997). This is all helpful, to me, in reflecting on the historical, cultural-material and political place from which I write as a legal scholar.

[5] For an overview of some of these, see Shone & Stonard, 2013, particularly Stonard's 'Introduction'.

[6] See, for example, essays by Amelia Jones, Anne Balsam and Donna Haraway in Mirzoeff, 2002.

Exemplarity Studies, Not-theory and Knowing the Example

I often end up with at least one 'oblique' question or focus for a piece of writing that sits parallel to the ostensible one and informs how I approach it. Perhaps this allows me to address the complexity of subject matter, or the generative potential of the 'space between' academic *topoi*. Adding another thematic question or focus might seem to double the volume of relevant debates, but paradoxically it narrows the operative terrain by identifying a clear point of intersection. In this case, the above framing would make this a chapter about the specific exemplarity of the body as a problem of representation, and vice versa.

There is a wealth of legal commentary, criticism and philosophy addressing the notion of exemplarity. Some of it takes a wider disciplinary and historical frame that integrates legal themes; some focuses more directly on law or normativity (see Lowrie & Lüdemann, 2015; Condello, 2018, 2020). This work will provide a major background against which I will write, offering useful readings of key texts that I can build on (or against). It's also relatively less impossible that some of these authors may end up reading my piece, which would encourage me to think in terms of a dialogue with or response to one or more of them. I would make sure that the theme of the 'hypothetical' special issue, as well as my focus on techniques, methodology and ontologies of representation, are at the front of my mind. The theme helps me to figure out which parts of this work are most useful, and where I might add to it. A technique I often use to make this easier, especially where I share a lot of common ground with the existing literatures, is to ask not what those literatures are *saying*, but what they are *doing*. My framing seems to depart from a dominant strand of this work, which is oriented to determining the nature of the example as far as law is concerned, underlining exemplarity's function in constituting, maintaining or operating an entity augured into being under the name 'the Law'. This literature often draws on Giorgio Agamben's notion of the 'paradigm' and the 'exemplary' in his method (see especially Agamben, 2009), in order to present a 'critical' account of legal ontology, make a normative argument that favours singularity and particularity, or historically locate treatments of exemplarity and connect them to paradigms of judgment (see Ferrara, 2008; Goodrich, 2015). Yet, in talking *about* exemplarity rather than absorbing it as a methodological principle, these literatures can seem to treat law as an object or practice that is separate from the authors as legal scholars, and knowing and acting subjects. By contrast, the emphasis of my piece would be to discuss in detail how a particular representation of the body 'works', while reflexively addressing my own presentation of the example as a different use of that methodological and rhetorical strategy. While this might involve drawing on technical legal and normative dimensions, I aim to keep generalisations to a minimum. I would avoid auguring 'Law' into being *a priori*, by attributing it with causal agency in relation to my example. In this sense, Agamben's work might present a concrete point of departure from these other 'legal' approaches. As he writes, his goal is less to theorise the paradigm of the exemplary for its 'normative effects' (Agamben, 2002), and more to 'pursue' a particular 'model of knowledge' (Agamben, 1993, pp. xv–xviii). For me, his methodological writing is better understood not (only) as a framework for describing 'what law is or does', but as the articulation of a concrete strategy for acculturating alternative ontologies.

In other words, where much of the literature appears as 'theoretical' with respect to its object, I would intend my chapter as an experiment in scholarship that is a praxis with an immediately political and ethical status. As well as being *about* something, academic analysis and writing *is itself* something. For Michel Foucault and Gilles Deleuze, 'theory' is, 'within a larger sphere', also an action that acts as a relay and forms networks (Foucault & Deleuze, 1977, pp. 206–207). Since my chapter's 'sphere' is epistemological praxes as forms of intellectual and social 'conduct', it collapses the 'about something' and 'is something' registers into each other. A similar idea has been proposed in the field of art criticism to point to the shift from artists understanding their work as imaginary or utopian to 'actually be[ing] ways of living and models of action within the existing real' (Bourriaud, 2002, p. 13). In the realm of intellectual method using examples, Jacques Rancière helpfully claims that 'a method means a path'—but 'not the path that a thinker follows', rather the path they *construct*, via the 're-staging of a limited number of ... scenes or events of discourse' (which are, similarly, particular examples or cases) (Rancière, 2009, pp. 114, 117). Rancière's aim is not to 'produce a theory of politics, aesthetics, literature, cinema or anything else' from these examples, but to characterise the immediate contemporary situation in which he finds himself, how a particular set of ideas are materially produced, and what work they are doing in a specific context. In the legal academy, Shaun McVeigh similarly sidesteps the 'theoretical' denotation, emphasising the jurisprudent as the active recipient of a tradition of thought, understood as a 'training in conduct for office'. McVeigh's 'shift' has been described as a concrete 'practice, craft and ethos' (Chalmers & Pahuja, 2021) that takes up the responsibility for maintaining (lawful) social relations (McVeigh, 2015, 2017: and he also addresses bodies, in a piece on the repatriation of human remains, McVeigh, 2014). For me this understanding of legal scholarship is significant, given the 'profound impact' that jurisprudence has always had on the development of the law (see Gordley, 2014).

As far as writing a short book chapter on the body goes, these considerations quickly become an unwieldy collection of understandings of intellectual work. Still, an aim for this piece would be to challenge myself to articulate my methodology and, according to its precepts, make clear the substantive inseparability of subject, technique and object. Agamben's work offers an economical way to combine the elements at play here—epistemological praxis, the body and the modern representational political ontology that is central to modern law and political authority (Loughlin, 2004, ch 4; see also Fenichel Pitkin, 1972; Kantorowicz, 1997; Esposito, 2015). Agamben has addressed 'the body' directly,[7] but my focus would be on his discussion of exemplarity, and the connection with his treatment of Walter Benjamin's method. In 1977, he proposed Benjamin's 'criticism' as a bridge between philosophical knowledge and poetic representation: it 'neither represents nor knows, but knows the representation' (Agamben, 1993, p. xvii). Sigrid Weigel, separately, analysed Benjamin's method through the notion of a 'body and image space', exploring the centrality of 'thinking-in-images' (Weigel, 1996) and non-representational 'constellations' (see Benjamin, 2019). Working through an example of the body using this framing, I would hope to move beyond *describing* an alternative to representational political ontologies or *diagnosing* the intertwining of nomos and physis that this paradigm entails.

With these pieces in place, I would (finally) survey existing work on law and the body that engages with these themes or literatures. I would revisit landmark works in feminist-led investigations of representation, the body and law; older classics like Cheah, Fraser and Grbich's *Thinking Through the Body of the Law* (1996), Mari Matsuda's *Where Is Your Body?* (1997), as well as more recent publications such as Martin Kayman's work, Hosman and Korsten's special issue of *Law and Literature* (2016) on 'Legal Bodies: Corpus/Persona/Communitas', and Griffin and Danil's 'Law's Changing Bodies: Contemporary and Historical Perspectives on Law and Embodiment' (2019) in the *Australian Feminist Law Journal.*

Choosing an Example

It might be easy to imagine that choosing an example is a matter of finding something that illustrates this approach. This is exactly what I would try to avoid. An 'example' in this sense is not an illustration of a pre-formed theory, it is something that asserts itself and asks to be taken more seriously. It detains the mind's gaze, asking to be 'thought with', rather than thought about. In the past I have chosen examples by intuition, discovering them more by chance encounter than through the literatures of my field or a specific sphere of practice. I test their potential by thinking about them in terms of my broad intellectual orientations and interests, but if their intrigue or significance can be mapped out quickly then I don't need to write about them. Typically, before accepting an invitation to contribute to an edited volume, I would already have a candidate example that the volume will allow me to exorcise. An intellectual hoarder, I keep paper scraps, flyers, notes, references and electronic lists of the various things I encounter that 'interest' me. But 'interest' is too mild—I keep things from any academic discipline or cultural milieu that 'jolt' me, that resonate strongly with current projects, nagging involuntary thoughts, or cultural patterns I sense emerging. I never look at these piles and lists (except when cleaning up or moving, when I have no idea where to put them), but I figure that the 'sticky' ones come to mind at the right time.

[7] Agamben (2016), as well as several more oblique addresses to the body.

My example is likely to be 'contemporary'. I enjoy the tradition of re-reading 'classic' figures in order to highlight contemporary contours of thought—like Antigone, or St Paul—but I would not attempt this for a chapter that is tangential to my research programme. I admire the historical turn in legal studies, but I have no flair for or training in history and feel unqualified to try my hand. I have preferred using examples that initially seem 'self-evident' or 'commonplace' (including legal examples) that don't require specialist information to understand. I enjoy giving these examples extraordinary attention and carefully 'working' them, so that they show their historical roots and the longer patterns that they make uniquely visible. It's important to me that the objects be unique—though they may not appear as such initially. However, thinking again of my past work, I have never believed that a 'non-specialist' understanding is wrong or should be set aside. Rather, it is part of the example and of what the example means in its context.

I don't usually draw sharp distinctions between 'legal' and 'non-legal' examples, but which one I choose can have practical consequences for the process and potential argument. Where I have taken a legal example, the focus has been to show how ordering normative principles are mutually contingent on material and textual practices. For example, my analysis of the 'thumbprint evidence' in the Australian stolen generations litigation showed how the principle of sovereignty and concrete interpretative and evidentiary practices are in a reinforcing relation (Parsley, 2006). One does not *cause* the other: politico-legal conditions are acculturated by both conceptual-abstract structures, and practical techniques, constraints, choices and priorities. One approach here might be to select an example of how a legal process represents and positions a body to 'make it appear' in a particular instance. Although this looks close to what I wanted to avoid in the 'exemplarity' literature, it would enable me to foreground the tension between the rhetorical presentation of the body as natural and the techniques by which this effect is achieved—something I have addressed (differently) in recent work on juridical craft and personhood (Mussawir & Parsley, 2017). I'm wondering particularly about the importance of working bodies in the context of digital platforms and labour law—but although I think a lot about artificial intelligence and political economy, I'd need to spend more time with this material to see if I could find something appropriate.

The alternative would be to choose a 'non-legal' example. Although I have sometimes analysed things that other legal scholars might think (or tell me that they do think) are irrelevant to law, for me there was always an essential cultural, political, ontological or indeed methodological connection—and the success of the work depends on articulating it. Whereas in my earlier work I was concerned to bring law's apparent externalities within it—knowledge, disciplines, creativity—I don't think much in terms of this 'topography' now, though I'm aware it's still central to accounts of legality. I would prefer to frame a more general issue about pervasive cultural technologies of representation and representationalism, shared between 'life' and 'law', that help *this* law to belong to *this* life. Legal techniques, that is, can themselves be 'exemplary' in relation to broader patterns (see also Antaki, 2020).

An obvious path for me would be to expand on earlier work that addresses adjacent themes. I have analysed the representation of 'the animal' in cinema, and in political and legal theory, showing how the structures and conventions of visualisation, viewing and narrative relate to both a 'pathos' for animality and political ontologies of personhood (Parsley, 2013). I focused on an Armenian film, Harutyun Khachatryan's *Border* (2009), but I've been meaning to compare an older film, Robert Bresson's *Au Hasard Balthasar*, and a newer one, Bong Joon-ho's *Okja*. This would involve some reaching though; analogising animality to the body, which doesn't appeal to me. I might make a more lateral move to Chantal Akerman's 1975 classic *Jeanne Dielman, 23 quai du Commerce, 1080 Bruxelles*, often analysed in terms of time, labour and social reproduction. To return to the labour law speculation, I might wonder about representations of the bodies of gig economy or Amazon workers, whom I think about a lot and who have been the subject of litigation. Internet searching, including image searching, would be a first port of call to see if my hunch has paid off, followed by academic literature searches to see if anyone else has been writing about this. I would be interested to observe differences and commonalities in the work done by particular constructions of the body—contrasting media and law, or historicising them in terms of the major visual cultural tradition that analyses the representation of work and labour.

Still on 'labour' but in a different way, recently one of my 'stickiest' cultural examples has been the work of American artist Cameron Rowland. Since I saw his *D37* exhibition in Los Angeles in 2018, I have been using it in my teaching. *D37* is a collection of works that show with clinical, barristerial precision how overlapping legal mechanisms from property, criminal law, taxation and local housing law harmonise with economic practices to produce systemic racial inequality. Rowland's work is 'exemplary' in the sense of being exceptional, while embodying what are, to me, important aspects of contemporary art. These include the convergence of critical jurisprudential thinking and research with artistic practice; the use of legal materials in constructing artworks or leveraging the legal status of a practice or material to endow the artwork with its meaning or effect; the anti-aesthetic movement in art; new frontiers of institutional critique and the interrogation of the economic-political history of the exhibiting institutions; and the reworking of the politics-art nexus. Rowland's later show, *3 & 4 Will. IV c. 73* at the Institute of Contemporary Art (ICA) in London in 2020, similarly, forensically reconstructs the interplay of legal and economic reason and technique after the passing of the 'Act for the Abolition of Slavery throughout the British Colonies; for promoting the Industry of the manumitted Slaves; and for compensating the Persons hitherto entitled to the Services of such Slaves, 1833'. Their effect, he argues, is to 'preserve the property established by slavery'. On display are material objects that are actual contemporary examples of such property that have become literally 'part of the furniture'. What might qualify one or both these shows for this hypothetical chapter is that their searing account of the embedded heredity of slavery in contemporary racial inequality is achieved without any representation of people or bodies whatsoever. Rowland exhibits objects and documents: bikes (property) confiscated from kids, titles to land, covenant documents, mortgage details, the ICA's doors and handrails. This isn't what I originally had in mind. That might be fine, but it might force me to explore absence-presence issues that are central to the iconographic tradition and could become fairly tedious or obvious. On the other hand, perhaps my enthusiasm for Rowland's work will let me find a new angle on those well-worn issues, enabling me to talk about a lot of things I find important.

Writing with the Example

In a sense, the process of selecting an example is the first stage of 'writing', since many of the broadest brush strokes are figured out during that process. As outlined above, at that point I might have intuitions about the elements of the analysis—some basic idea of what is important about the example and what I think it shows, or would enable (or force) me to say. With the example 'sticking' in my mind, ideas for how to structure the chapter or fragments of the analysis would occur to me involuntarily before I really start working on it. In this case, several alternative structures would occur to me as I process how I need to approach the various components.

Once writing is underway, the researching and structuring process is not over but changes form. Writing is incremental and circular, involving various stages of research, reading, ideating/analysing, structuring and drafting. Eventually, it tends to 'click', and I can 'write out' the piece, but only after several stints of further research, rearranging, rewriting. Sometimes this research is very targeted (e.g. if I realise I need to work with the etymology of a particular word, understand an artist's wider output better, or see how a discipline has handled a particular problem). Importantly, this research is not about finding a 'gap in the literature'—a key idea in many disciplines. Rather, it's about what new or further analysis this research makes possible or impossible to me, given my 'constellation' of factors.

Reading the most important texts is equal parts 'research' and 'writing', and it too has an involuntary dimension. It will tend to catalyse a rush of thoughts and (sometimes unrelated) plans for writing that it's hard to keep up with, especially in this case as I would be confronting a theme (the body) and methodological question that are hooked into my prior thinking. This usually happens the *first* time I read or watch something. Towards the end of my undergraduate studies, I got a copy of Damien Hirst's *On the Way to Work* (2001), which was influential for how I thought about making academic work. Hirst's mantra was (is?) 'first thought, best thought'. I don't know if my first thought is always my best one, and, of course, I repeat-watch and -read key materials. But often initial reactions and responses are when I'm clearest about what I need to say, or when I most clearly notice where my mind goes and how it joins things together.

This begets a writing problem, because even (or especially?) the most clearly felt connections can be hard to transpose into a necessarily linear text or reconcile with initial structure ideas. No matter how sure I am about things, they can change or move around in the writing process. Something I initially thought of as a section or paragraph can become a single line or a footnote, or vice versa, as the craft of telling the story—usually with hypothetical readers in mind—forces me to confront the particularities of the 'constellation'. This could come as an unexpected resonance between sources, a particularly arresting phrase, a need to acknowledge greater complexity in key literature, or being struck by a previously overlooked detail. It could generate a new textual device (like the title of a section, or a solution for joining otherwise disparate ideas). Other times it can dramatically change the claims I make, as happened while writing about the film *Border*. While re-watching the film during the writing process, I suddenly noticed a scene where the protagonist of the film (a buffalo) looks straight down the camera lens. This precipitated a crucial part of the analysis, on different modes of gaze in relation to cinematic craft. There, careful attention to detail married with a set of problems, ideas and 'theoretical' frameworks to create something new that emerged from the particularity of the example itself. I already 'understood' all the component parts, but their resonant potential only came together in the working out.

I would expect this hypothetical chapter to be a difficult process of dwelling with a set of curated materials that may (or may not) form a specific constellation in resonant ways. It's easy to imagine a dialectic between 'example' and 'analysis'; checking one against the other, repeatedly reconsidering the example then returning to the 'page'. But this is a bit too simple, since it doesn't usually feel so binary. It might be better to say that, at different points, any element can be the heuristic lens through which the spectrum of other elements appears. I like this image because it often does feel like an experiment in trying to see from multiple points of view, like a thriller where the audience observes fragmentary or conflicting versions of an event.

Yet, even if all the elements of the constellation are therefore important, the guiding aim of the writing process is to do justice to the example. This means something different (more?) than not making factual, legal or historical errors. It means putting the example into a framing that opens it up, revealing detail, nuance, significance, or, as I said above, its participation in broader or longer patterns that it makes uniquely visible. The writing shouldn't force it to carry conceptual weight it can't bear. Rather, the 'articulation' process should make the example *more itself*, by using whatever frameworks help to understand it more concertedly. Though it's certainly not 'top-down', like working up a 'case study' to illustrate a pre-formed analysis, this kind of writing is not entirely 'bottom-up' either, since I would have relatively clear (but malleable) ideas of why I'm looking at the example in the first place. Ideally, by the end of the writing process I (and hopefully the reader) would see *both* the example *and* the ideational aspects of the analysis differently, for having 'articulated' the two together. This might seem quite far from any substantive consideration of the body. Yet, for me, what this reflection and method opens up is precisely a connection with how the body tends to appear as just such a self-evident presence or unity, despite being a complex cultural-technical production (or 'informational pattern' as some disciplines might prefer to call it).

I'm also interested in the play of subjectivity and objectivity in a writing process like this, as another aspect of 'getting underneath' this self-evidence. I would intend my analysis to be not only rational and correct in its particulars, but resonant enough that the links it draws and the colouration it supplies 'can't be unseen'. I don't mean that I would aim to 'discover the truth' of the example in a historical or factual sense. Just as in the legal presentation of the example, different and contradictory accounts will be possible under someone else's hand. I would try to 'work' the constellation to discover the limit points of what I can say about it. I only partially experience this as a subjective or intentional process, since most of the time what I say seems inevitable to me—as if it is an inherent feature of the example itself rather than something added by my analysis (I think this relates to how I experience bodies, too). At other times, what I may want to say is constrained by the example, making me adjust my language until it 'unlocks' what I'm seeing. Even my own writing constrains me, in that, once I have some of the text down it becomes another source to respond to, remain consistent with, or push further. In this sense, I often think about my work as making an argument that's halfway between the way a lawyer makes a case and an artist makes an artwork. Neither is as objective or subjective (respectively?) as people tend to imagine. In their different ways, both have to negotiate the limits and directionality of media and materials, with 'ends' in mind that may or may not be reachable. Both 'stress test' their discourse and materials to find the limits of what they can do. Both find out, after the fact, what was or wasn't possible under that hand, at that time, with those materials, in that context.

A final important consideration is the play of subjectivity and objectivity 'within' the example. Each representation of the body is itself the same kind of negotiation that I have just described. This is a well-charted issue in literary, aesthetic and media cultural analysis: techniques and forms mediate the agency of an instigator or author in myriad ways. Bodies, too, as well as their subjects, might have a particular kind of agency or resistance within the specific example. The legal context is a fraught one for these issues. Authors can be tempted either to attribute agency to law, or attribute 'lawness' to ideas, motivations, or effects of a cultural object. This can often be a function of the analysis rather than the example: some legal scholars look for 'Law' everywhere and never fail to find it. I hope not to do this. First, as mentioned above, I would not frame my work as an investigation about law as such. Second, I would avoid any claims of causation (e.g. about the underlying causes of an instance of representation, or what it causes in its viewers including in me), which would require documentary, qualitative or quantitative support depending on the claim being made. I have sometimes referred to authorial intent, but only as one contributing factor (rather than the truth of the representation) and only where I can quote a reliable source or interview. Third, like Foucauldian approaches, critical theory and legal and media studies, I would pay more attention to the *conditions* that make the example possible, formal and conceptual structures, or what it reveals or allows us to see and say. Finally, I would try to make the narrowest claims possible, ensuring they are supported by things I can evidence directly. These issues can all arise at the level of individual statements, but avoiding them successfully is mainly a function of the overall framing of the piece. Ultimately, the author establishes and controls the rhetorical space within which some kinds of claim acquire gravitas or become beside the point. Even so, different disciplinary audiences may chafe at these convictions—for example, peer reviewers in cultural studies once required me to reference 'audience reception' literature, even though I believed I had made it irrelevant in my framing and claims. In the edited collection context though, there might be more understanding and leeway from editors.

At a decisive moment in the writing process, it will be time to give the piece its title. This is a very helpful exercise, in which I reflect seriously on what it is I'm really doing and saying, and which components need a place in the phrase that will represent the work to the world. This is about divining the soul of the piece. Sometimes it makes me realise that what I *should* do is different from what I have been doing. It's also a question of figuring out how I would like other people to see the work, and what search terms should locate it. It's important to try and signal what's going on in the work *beyond* presenting the example—which might otherwise unduly restrict the audience. Again, the edited collection context takes some pressure off, as the piece will appear as part of a volume alongside other contributions, benefitting from their framing and themes.

Conclusion

Thinking and writing through a single example has been an important method for me at particular moments in my research. I have often considered individual cultural or legal representations in relation to ordering concepts and political ontologies. The chance to write a book chapter on 'the body' would extend both of these dimensions. On the one hand, in pushing me to formalise my method it would enable a more overt reflection on the epistemological qualities of my own scholarship and ethos. On the other, it would allow me to consider the 'exemplary' status of the body, as a case 'par excellence' of the way technical practices and representational cultures figure 'natural' matter within determinate processes and for particular ends. Depending on the example chosen, the emphasis of this chapter might be on highlighting the way a particular technique functions. It might call a legal or political process to account by contributing to knowledge about it. It might point to features of—or changing conditions within—a more general political ontology or media culture. Either way, in addition to the above reasons, I am drawn to this method because it involves trying to 'do justice' to an object, experienced as an enabling constraint on the subjective process of drawing things into a specific constellation, which seems especially appropriate for writing about the body. This might allow me to draw multi-layered connections between legal practices and scholarly ones, and between the subjects of epistemological practices and the objects of their representations. I would hope that this might add something to contemporary considerations of methods and methodology, modelling how techniques that have been central to legal thinking can be repurposed as methods in interdisciplinary cultural studies, with the aim of counter-reading or opening things up to new potential understandings. Ideally, this might help articulate a conception of methodology that could be useful to others working with humanities approaches in the legal setting.

The choice to work with a single example has at times enabled me to write when I was overwhelmed by complexity, literatures and possibilities. It also comes with significant limits and is not always a good choice. Writing this way ties thinking to a very restricted subject. It often means that the background and (inter)disciplinary knowledge that make the analysis possible don't have an overt place within it, since it is limited to 'material' considerations. This inhibits the kind of field-organising and positioning work that is more widely discovered, read and used. But, at its best, it can demonstrate how concerted, careful attention to particular things can transform both habitual conceptual framing, and those things themselves.

References

Agamben, G. (1993). *Stanzas: Word and Phantasm in Western Culture* (R. L. Martinez, trans., pp. xv–xviii). University of Minnesota Press.

Agamben, G. (2002). *What is a Paradigm?* Lecture delivered at the European Graduate School. Retrieved 9 August 2021 from https://www.youtube.com/watch?v=G9Wxn1L9Er0

Agamben, G. (2009). What is a Paradigm? In *The Signature of All Things: On Method* (L. D'Isanto with K. Attell, trans.). Zone Books.

Agamben, G. (2016). *The Use of Bodies* (A. Kotsko, trans.). Stanford University Press.

Antaki, M. (2020). Exemplarity and the Resonance of Reasoning. In A. Condello (Ed.), *New Rhetorics for Contemporary Legal Discourse*. Edinburgh University Press.

Baudrillard, J. (2007). *Forget Foucault*. Semiotexte.

Benjamin, W. (2019). *Origin of the German Trauerspiel* (H. Eiland, trans.). Harvard University Press.

Bourriaud, N. (2002). *Relational Aesthetics* (S. Pleasance & F. Woods with M. Copeland, trans.). Les Presses Du Real.

Chalmers, S., & Pahuja, S. (2021). Introduction—Practice, Craft and Ethos: Inheriting a Tradition. In S. Chalmers & S. Pahuja (Eds.), *The Routledge Handbook of International Law and the Humanities*. Routledge.

Cheah, P., Fraser, D., & Grbich, J. (1996). *Thinking Through the Body of the Law*. Allen & Unwin.

Condello, A. (2018). *Between Ordinary and Extraordinary: The Normativity of the Singular Case in Art and Law*. Brill.
Condello, A. (2020). *New Rhetorics for Contemporary Legal Discourse*. Edinburgh University Press.
Constable, M. (1994). Genealogy and Jurisprudence: Nietzsche, Nihilism, and the Social Scientification of Law. *Law and Social Inquiry, 19*, 551.
Esposito, R. (2015). *Categories of the Impolitical* (C. Parsley, trans.). Fordham University Press.
Fenichel Pitkin, H. (1972). *The Concept of Representation*. University of California Press.
Ferrara, A. (2008). *The Force of the Example: Explorations in the Paradigm of Judgment*. Columbia University Press.
Foucault, M., & Deleuze, G. (1977). Intellectuals and Power. In D. F. Bouchard (Ed.), *Language, Counter-Memory, Practice: Selected Essays and Interviews*. Cornell University Press.
Goodrich, P. (2015). The Exampleless Example: Of the Infinite Particulars of Early Modern Common Law. In M. Lowrie & S. Lüdemann (Eds.), *Exemplarity and Singularity: Thinking through Particulars in Philosophy, Literature and Law*. Routledge.
Gordley, J. (2014). *The Jurists: A Critical History*. Oxford University Press.
Griffin, L., & Danil, L. R. (2019). Law's Changing Bodies: Contemporary and Historical Perspectives on Law and Embodiment. *Australian Feminist Law Journal, 45*(1), 1–4.
Groys, B. (2016). *Particular Cases*. Sternberg Press.
Hirst, D. (2001). *On the Way to Work*. Faber & Faber.
Hosman, Y., & Korsten, F.-W. (Eds.). (2016). *Law and Literature, 28*(3). Special issue on 'Legal Bodies: Corpus/Persona/Communitas'.
Julius, A. (2003). *Transgressions: The Offences of Art*. University of Chicago Press.
Kantorowicz, E. H. (1997). *The King's Two Bodies*. Princeton University Press.
Kohn, E. (2013). *How Forests Think: Toward an Anthropology Beyond the Human*. University of California Press.
Law, J. (2004). *After Method: Mess in Social Science Research*. Routledge.
Loughlin, M. (2004). *The Idea of Public Law*. Oxford University Press.
Lowrie, M., & Lüdemann, S. (Eds.). (2015). *Exemplarity and Singularity: Thinking Through Particulars in Philosophy, Literature and Law*. Routledge.
Manderson, D. (2015). Bodies in the Water: On Reading Images More Sensibly. *Law and Literature, 27*(2), 279.
Matsuda, M. J. (1997). *Where Is Your Body?: And Other Essays on Race, Gender, and the Law*. Beacon Press.
McVeigh, S. (2014). Law as (More or Less) Itself: On Some not Very Reflective Elements of Law. *University of California Irvine Law Review, 4*, 471.
McVeigh, S. (2015). Afterword: Office and the Conduct of the Minor Jurisprudent. *University of California Irvine Law Review, 5*, 499.
McVeigh, S. (2017). Office and Persona of the Critical Jurist: Peripheral Legal Thought (Australia). In J. Desautels-Stein & C. Tomlins (Eds.), *Searching for Contemporary Legal Thought*. Cambridge University Press.
Mirzoeff, N. (Ed.). (2002). *The Visual Culture Reader* (2nd ed.). Routledge.
Murphy, T. (1997). *The Oldest Social Science? Configurations of Law and Modernity*. Oxford University Press.

Mussawir, E., & Parsley, C. (2017). The Law of Persons Today: At the Margins of Jurisprudence. *Law and Humanities, 11*(1), 44.
Parsley, C. (2003). Performing the Border: Australia's Judgment of Unauthorised Arrivals at the Airport. *Australian Feminist Law Journal, 18*, 55.
Parsley, C. (2006). Seasons in the Abyss: Reading the Void in *Cubillo*. In A. Orford (Ed.), *International Law and Its Others*. Cambridge University Press.
Parsley, C. (2013). The Animal Protagonist: Representing 'the Animal' in Law and Cinema. In E. Mussawir & Y. Otomo (Eds.), *Law and the Question of the Animal*. Routledge.
Rancière, J. (2009). A Few Remarks on the Method of Jacques Rancière. *Parallax, 15*(3), 114.
Riles, A. (2005). *A New Agenda for the Cultural Study of Law: Taking on the Technicalities*. Cornell Faculty Law Publications Paper 782.
Rush, P. (1997). An Altered Jurisdiction: Corporeal Traces of Law. *Griffith Law Review, 6*, 144.
Sherwin, R. (2012). Visual Jurisprudence. *New York University Law Review, 56*, 137.
Shone, J.-P., & Stonard, R. (2013). *The Books that Shaped Art History: From Gombrich and Greenberg to Alpers and Krauss*. Thames & Hudson.
Sugarman, D. (1992). A Hatred of Disorder: Legal Science, Liberalism and Imperialism. In P. Fitzpatrick (Ed.), *Dangerous Supplements: Resistance and Renewal in Jurisprudence*. Pluto Press.
Toracca, T. (2008). Towards Exemplarity: When the Particular Matters. *Law and Literature, 30*, 465.
Viveiros de Castro, E. (2014). *Cannibal Metaphysics*. University of Minnesota Press.
Weigel, S. (1996). *Body- and Image-Space: Re-reading Walter Benjamin*. Routledge.
Young, A. (1998). The Waste Land of the Law, the Wordless Song of the Rape Victim. *Melbourne University Law Review, 22*(2), 442.

Cases

Mabo v Queensland (No 2) (1992) 175 CLR 1, 28, Brennan CJ.
R v Brown [1993] 2 All ER 75.

CHAPTER 8

~~Cross-Disciplinarity as a Practice of Critical Linking: How Does a Scholar Relate Different 'Bodies'~~? Writing from Within the Body as a Research Process

Hyo Yoon Kang

Abstract Legal academic writing seldom reflects on its choice of research topic and writing style. The published text rarely incorporates thoughts about the choice of genre or format, and their fit with the research question itself. This chapter observes its own pre-writing process rather than making an argument or a claim as most academic writings do. An injury made me discard my initial plan for the chapter, and the notion of the 'body', which the editors had assigned me as the object of a hypothetical interdisciplinary study, became the material subject of the writing process itself. Experiencing bodily constraints changed my reading practice and necessitated different media and writing strategies. The resulting text is a personal record of reading and thinking in a particular period of time.

Keywords Body • Pain • Writing • Auto-research • Interdisciplinarity

And were it true, we do not think all philosophy is worth one hour of pain.
—Blaise Pascal, *Pensées*, A Dutton, New York (1958): section 79. Retrieved August 26, 2021, from *https://www.gutenberg.org/files/18269/18269-0.txt*

H. Y. Kang (✉)
University of Kent, Canterbury, UK
e-mail: h.y.kang@kent.ac.uk

D. Herman, C. Parsley (eds.), *Interdisciplinarities*, Palgrave Socio-Legal Studies, https://doi.org/10.1007/978-3-030-89297-5_8

Introduction (Written Later, 15 November 2020)

This is a diaristic record of the process of finding anew an argument for a hypothetical chapter on the 'body'. The reason for the unusual format is that my own body became the subject rather than the object of this exercise in academic thinking about methodology. The novelist Elias Khoury (2017) said: 'I try not to write about war, but to write from within it.' Similarly, this piece would be better described as a writing from within the body rather than about it.

This chapter records the inchoate impressions from initial readings and other materials loosely related to the 'body' that had caught my eye in autumn 2020. The circumstances that led to these readings began much earlier in late January 2020 when I had started following news about the novel 'Chinese' virus and observed the subsequent incidents of anti-Asian racism and revelations of character in my closest personal circles. As the initial brief was to show the 'working out' of an interdisciplinary writing process, I decided to leave my entries in disconnected sequence and edited them only lightly (except the one from voice transcription) because I did not want to mould them into a single controlled narrative. This format more candidly reflects the fluctuating thoughts on a theme that is so deeply and widely discussed and written about as the one in question, namely the body. Such haphazard thoughts help to find out what exactly it is that bothers me about something (e.g. misrepresentations, fissures within legal conceptual premises, simplistic interpretations, accepted 'truths', sloppy definitions, argumentative cowardice, analytical shortcuts). Figuring out a problematisation is, for me, the most joyful part of research. At that stage, the thinking process leading up to a piece of research is still wide open, and I learn a lot by reading about what I don't know.

On this particular occasion, the chapter's gestational process was more disorganised than at other times. I had an initial plan, but I felt ill at ease with it and could not rekindle interest in it. I abandoned it and started thinking and figuring out from scratch again. This might have to do with the reassessment of research, or even life, priorities and ways of doing research at the start of a global pandemic. More personally, my aversion to the initial plan stemmed from an injury. It developed during the first lockdown and is still ongoing. The various limitations imposed by my body, as well as the pandemic lockdowns, changed my ability to navigate everyday life. As many of our bodies were confined in interior worlds during this pandemic year, my own bodily trapping felt like an additional layer of the world of interior.

What was different about these different kinds of locked-down interiorities, however, was that the collective experience of a pandemic was at odds with the private nature of an injury that could not be communicated and addressed because of the non-availability of medical treatment during the first lockdown. Perhaps my body chose to react to this year's turmoil by turning on itself as if it was trying to surpass the emotional interruptions caused by the pandemic by providing me with a physical distraction.

My bodily exterior does not show pain except when I move in a certain way. But within the bodily interior, pain's domination is near absolute. It demands immediate undivided attention like an emperor, overriding my will to ignore it. My body tells me when I can work and when I cannot. Pain is its messenger. So, in a way I have been left with no other choice but to try to write *with* the body, or from *within* the body, rather than *about* the body.

* * *

Speaking or writing about the relation between my personal body or life and research or work is something that I have declined in the past. I have felt the emotional labour of researching matters close to my own life too burdensome and sensitive. Sometimes, I also thought that to do so may be self-indulgent. I didn't want my assigned identity to be dictating my research. Yet, what the pandemic orientalism and anti-Asian and anti-Black racism showed me this year was that the process of academic research and writing often compartmentalises and conceals the number of personae that we have developed over time for different social settings by dislocating and erasing the 'I' from academic texts. This is not a new insight. Many academic texts have attempted to incorporate the process of writing into the published work (e.g. Kathleen Stewart, Lauren Berlant, Katherine McKittrick). For me it was the pandemic that laid bare the limits of my attempt to separate my academic and private personae. I could not exclude my own bodily experience whilst thinking about and preparing for this assignment which was asking me how I would go about writing about the 'body'.

Much of academic research presumes the researcher's ability to recognise, understand and present different perspectives, and the writing process is supposed to be one of judicious deliberation. The most interesting academic research involves a kind of queering against the grain of accepted norms; presenting a novel perspective by exposing the strangeness of the taken-for-granted beliefs and practices. This kind of unsettling can take the form of deconstruction and critique, or also historicisation. Interdisciplinary scholarship appears to be valued for the introduction of another point of view than one's own. Also meta-discourses about ways of knowing and specific constructions of truth-claims serve to show the limits and peculiarities of a particular knowledge tradition and the difficulty of these different ways of knowing to communicate and understand each other. My past scholarship, for example, tried to work out a notion of materiality specific to law or problematised reductionist representations of scientific knowledge in legal settings (Kang, 2012, 2018; Kang & Kendall, 2019).

But I started to wonder whether the presumption of possessing a distance or even the ability to understand the other fairly, not to mention the ability to see with multiple perspectives, especially in multi-disciplinary or cross-disciplinary research, is a privilege that the very subjects or objects of a research may sometimes be denied for themselves. For example, the objects of our research may be non-human organisms lacking a common language with us, or are dead, or they may be inorganic matter. Some living human objects of study are seen to lack objectivity or voice precisely for the reason that they feel pain, or are angry about injustice. Or they are not regarded as being humans of equal value and hence lack credible voice. Only few scholars have experienced or lived the realities of the situations they are describing. I remember Yael Berda, a sociologist, once asking how many international refugee law scholars have actually ever been to a refugee camp.[1]

Reductionist objectification can also occur through interdisciplinarity. Although it is often assumed to provide a richer perspective than from the viewpoint of a single discipline, interdisciplinarity can sometimes offer a novelty factor without putting in the effort to represent the other disciplinary tradition and its internal debates fully. Problems are presented as loose associations between different disciplinary 'views', which are in fact neither uniform nor uncontested within their 'home' disciplines. The result is one discipline exoticising the 'other'. The philosopher Reza Negarestani called this phenomenon a 'contemporary grift culture' which is enabled by the 'facility of a vague concept known as Interdisciplinarity. You can make a series of swindles in arts, humanities, science, etc by moving across the borders effectively' (today at @NegarestaniReza).[2]

Over the course of spring and summer, I felt tired of 'theorytalks' as a thing in itself, especially of big abstract concepts (e.g. biopower, necropolitics, Anthropocene, capitalism, sovereignty) and facile metaphorisations of the current, specific and diverse pandemic experiences (e.g. network, immunity, virality). I became wary of social theorists who handily 'applied' their existing ideas in order to explain a pandemic not previously experienced, little known about and still unfolding. These theorists moulded the world into their existing theoretical grid instead of seeing in what ways the latter can fit the current world, if at all. Such a practice could be called theoretical imperialism. To a certain degree, our vision is always shaped by what we have seen previously, but there has to be room to recognise the inbuilt possibility of error or excess, as Georges Canguilhem would say. The imperative theorists lacked any concrete or constructive suggestions to better the conditions of peoples' suffering. The abstract theorytalks contrasted starkly with the neighbourhood actions of mutual help during the first lockdown. From April onwards, I read novels, essays, biographies and autofictions as they seemed to me more immediate and truthful forms of writing. And so this chapter assignment became the starting point to think about a broader issue than interdisciplinary research methods, namely that of a research voice and purpose: why and how one should write about which questions.

* * *

[1] https://twitter.com/YaelBerda/status/1329816313133477888?s=20 accessed 26 August 2021.

[2] https://twitter.com/NegarestaniReza/status/1328010109759447040?s=20 accessed 26 August 2021.

Sometime in September 2020[3]

This chapter originates from an invitation to contribute to a volume on interdisciplinary methodology on the theme of the body. The chapter that I had initially proposed to the editors would have developed a distinction between interdisciplinary and cross- or multi-disciplinary approaches to the 'body'. I would have argued for the latter by critiquing vague interdisciplinarity, which facilitates superficial namedropping and misappropriation of concepts without a regard for their own specific histories of intradisciplinary debates. Such a broad-brush interdisciplinarity borrows another discipline's concepts and uproots them in order to make a point about a different set of problems in one's own home discipline. In this process, an idea or theory or concept may become reduced in its complexity or mispresented, but, in a different disciplinary context, it is seen as 'novel'. As the 'home' discipline does not know much about the 'novel' concept, there is no discussion of any potential misunderstandings or misrepresentations. There is also little visibility or interest from the other discipline from which an idea was borrowed, so misunderstandings cannot be corrected. Oftentimes, deeper conceptual explorations are also not desired as they would complicate things too much. Barbara Stafford wrote incisively about the potential benefits and pitfalls of analogies (2001).

Other problems of interdisciplinarity include dialogues not based on mutual openness (one side is more open than other; pretend dialogue for ethics-washing); deferring to the other's expertise with superficial knowledge of the other discipline; lack of rigour because of 'diplomatic' tact or humility that covers it up; and overemphasis on commonalities rather than differences. Such interdisciplinary issues were the reasons why I analysed the use of 'materiality' in legal scholarship and proposed a more differentiated meaning specific to legal scholarship. Genuine inter-, trans-, or even multi-disciplinarity is rare given the highly fragmented and specialised nature of academic knowledge and its organisation, not to mention the current demands of academic 'production' or 'output' depending on which environments we work in. So, my proposed chapter for this volume would have sketched one possible map of a cross-disciplinary exercise in which other disciplinary internal debates and disagreements would be represented, as well as one's own intradisciplinary traditions critically examined. It would have entailed lots of disciplinary crossings and uncertainties rather than the belief in the possibility of a lateral translation.

After the summer of 2020, and with the continuing Covid sadness, it has gotten to a point where the chapter that I wanted to write is not what matters to me the most right now. I am not even sure I am cognitively able to write it. With the injury and chronic pain, I am at the level of first-order observation, preoccupied with my own body as a feeling subject, rather than observing my

[3] This section is from my Otter AI online voice dictation app on my iPhone, which is stored in the cloud and then copied and pasted into Word. My voice provides a pitiable transcription, or rather the other way around. It needs a lot of corrections.

different disciplinary positions and usage of the 'body' as a concept (second order observation). At the moment, I feel an antipathy against anything which abstracises and diminishes from the physicality of the body. I need a more personal and direct writing than something. I don't know how to describe more precisely what I feel irritated about. It might be reading about the notion of 'body' in academic writing as an abstract object of analysis. Instead of writing about it in the abstract, I might as well observe myself and my body in this process towards the chapter writing. I am not sure how I would go about such a self-observation for an academic writing assignment. Also perhaps it is not a contradiction to my initial plan, but may add to it.

I could start learning more about the body feeling pain by reading some scholarly literature about it (after all this assignment is for a legal academic volume, and it ought to contain some scholarly sources, I tell myself). Perhaps it could help me figure out the exact reason for my irritation with meta-discourse at this moment.

* * *

28 September 2020

I remember a sunnily disposed friend telling me last year that someone is 'overly' obsessing over other people's stories of pain, as if that person was lacking a measured perspective and that focusing on others' pain was somehow improper or disproportionate. Does pain disappear when it is not paid attention to? Does it get better by brushing it aside? Which stories would we rather not hear and share? People talking about their pain are often uninteresting to those who cannot relate to them because they have not had the experience before, lack empathy, or are simply not interested. To others, listening to stories of illness and pain can also cause phantom pain when empathy is 'too' strong. I don't know what makes some people be more like one or the other.

I ordered Elaine Scarry's book *The Body in Pain: The Making and Unmaking of the World* (1985) after the summer when things were not going well health-wise. I wasn't sure whether I would be able to do desk-bound work again for a long time. Reading it, I was struck by her observation that the body is the boundary at which pain becomes unshareable. A person who sits next to someone cannot know how much pain the other person is in. It cannot be communicated in a direct way. In contrast to the state of speechlessness that she describes, Scarry's writing is meticulous and precise, and the depth of her analysis, particularly on the effects of torture on language and expression, is minutely methodical. For me, the key insight is: when we are in acute pain or we fall, we don't utter a word, but a sound escapes our mouth, a noise. I find myself thinking that this is very true and yet often forgotten in the language-centred practice of law and legal scholarship, namely that pain is that which escapes language. Also in reverse, not having a language is painful, sometimes perhaps even physically so. These observations imply that the body *is* the separation between the feeling subject (human or other sentient beings who feel pain) and its surrounding world.

Reading Scarry's emphasis on body's boundedness is refreshing. It helps me to see why being in pain is alienating and isolating despite popular theories of embodiment and cognitive sciences that argue that a body is social and permeable. Much of the research in the social and natural sciences over the last thirty years has focused on the connectedness and relationality between living organisms and their environments. Epigenetics is a prominent example of a discipline that is predicated on this kind of conceptual relationality, which queries the boundaries between inside/outside and individual lifespan/generational temporality. The trend to relate people, things, organic and inorganic entities into networks, assemblages, as well as tropes of 'becomings' and hybridity, was an understandable reaction against rigid binary divisions (mind/body; subject/object; nature/culture). Much of the literature that I had originally had in mind for this chapter claims connections between domains rather than delineating distinctions or divisions (Grosz, 1994; Haraway, 2007; Tsing, 2015). But reading Scarry makes me realise that the body's openness and permeability may apply more to healthy bodies or to bodies that are not in pain. It seems strange that some social models of relationality that stress the open porous relations of humans to their environment and becoming turn out to be unhelpful precisely when the body is in pain. On the other hand, theories of embodied cognition support Scarry's thesis (Damasio, 2003; Hayles, 2005). The body in pain affects the subject's ability to think and communicate.

Theories of distributed cognition and subjectivity do not seem to apply to bodies in pain because pain ties us to our world within (Clark, 1998; Rotman, 2008). My pain does not form part of an environment. It does not participate in networks. It cannot be shared by its very nature. (*Addendum*: one editor points out that the effects of my pain will affect my environment and people around me, even if not consciously or voluntarily shared by the person in pain. This makes me think that pain may exceed bodily boundary, but it's not felt and perceived in the same way) I think that these observations apply to both physical and emotional pain. When the body is in pain, there is an absoluteness of the separation of an individual body from the rest of the world. Pain is something which is so individual that it cannot be communicated as it is (one editor notes that this is very true of grief). The ability to communicate and to relate seems to stop at the threshold of pain. A body in pain is not, cannot be, social.

This assignment is turning into an experiment of documenting the process of writing in short fragments as long as I can write or dictate. Some people have a full outline before they start writing. Usually, I don't have a full outline, but I do generally think things through before writing. And then thoughts change again. Christoph Hoffmann has written about the research process that takes place within and through writing as 'desk research' (Hoffmann, 2013). When a problem or puzzle is complex and entangled, I usually have a theoretical step-by-step argument before starting to write. But the exact details of getting to a claim often arise during the writing process. Externalising thinking through inscription (or also through drawing) helps to map out the thinking process. The writing process may be different when one is writing about or presenting empirical studies because they are representations where the surveying or thinking has already occurred in a different format (e.g. surveys, quantitative methods). With theoretical work, writing helps me to think in logical steps. Sometimes it leads me to a very different ending than I expected at the beginning, or even wanted.[4]

Sometime After the Voice Recordings

It is difficult to think and write through voice. Writing has its own voice, which is not a sonorous one, at least not to me. More spatial, than temporal? I feel like I am losing my thought in the voice recordings. It just disappears. I'd rather try writing in short spurts, jot down thoughts.

1 October 2020

> Gradually remove from your experiential concept of the body everything that is empirical in it—the colour, the hardness or softness, the weight, even the impenetrability—there still remains the space that was occupied by the body (which has now entirely disappeared) and you cannot leave that out. (Kant)[5]

If I will lose the friend I had, because his memory is going in circles, or fading, and his persona seems to be a shade of what he was before, because of dementia or alcohol, he still gifts me the space that he occupied as a friend, but his body is not the friend that he was. I am not sure if the identity of the body deceives me, and himself, too.

Where does the body—person/I severance occur, if at all? I remember a friend telling me how a cremation was not a 'clean' way to be buried contrary to popular belief and how traumatised she was seeing the casket with her sibling's body being put into the furnace. She'd rather want to be buried in a contained space with the body 'intact', regardless of the fact whether it is alive or dead. The body would then still be within a specific space, and her children would know that's where the space of her body had once taken up.

7 October 2020

I was at the physio today. I am too distracted by the persistent pain, so that I don't feel able to connect any two, three (if they can be counted) thoughts and impressions together.

[4] Transcribed by https://otter.ai.

[5] *Critique of Pure Reason* (1998) Cambridge University Press: section B6, p 138.

Twitter format is strangely the only length of thought and typing (222 characters) that works fine for my current disabled upper body half and the resulting *Spatzenhirn*, a sparrow brain, which is the best description for my thinking capacity right now. My tweets today:

> A trumpian deja-vu when my physio said that i have 'internalised the covid'
> If i had a therapist, he'd say that i have 'externalised the covid'

I am not sure if my physio is right, but even if so, that does not change the pain, if not making it even worse.

14 October 2020

Since the pandemic and the injury, my languages are all mixed up in my head more than usual, and my current interior 'language' is none of them. It is, indeed, true, as Elaine Scarry writes: pain is that which escapes language. Dream feels most natural, as if I am more awake than in an awake state, a sentence pre-utterance or voicing is German, Korean, English, all mixed. Even single words come out mixed now. There is no 'official' me in 'me' able to be expressed by language at this point; only a very soft body.

15 October 2020

How this writing assignment is going:

> Getting started is partly stalling, stalling by way of reading and of listening to music. (Sontag, 2013)

No music, but reading unrelated books. Last book I read and loved? Maggie Nelson's *Argonauts* (2015). And Alexander Chee's *How to Write an Autobiographical Novel: Essays* (2018). I am worried that they are not the normal legal scholarly sources, but so many books are boring or irritating me at the moment. I don't have much time or patience; I can only bear acute writing that has urgency. I realise that the trade-off is truncation and a greater likelihood of leaving some stones unturned in this writing process, something which would have bothered me intensely in the past but no longer does because there are fewer things that matter right now.

16 October 2020

Saw this image in which people's heads stick out from a white sheet. It was a poster for 'bodies in crisis' of Anab Jain's Design Investigations Project (Fig. 8.1). I feel like I am in the photo.

Fig. 8.1 Design Investigations @D_I_Studio led by Anab Jain: "'BODIES IN CRISIS' Our winter brief explores how a crisis like COVID affects our bodies, our relationships and our spaces. As we drawing arm length circles of distance with other bodies, what do we need to do to be able to touch again and move through space with new intimacy?" 12 October 2020 https://twitter.com/D_I_Studio/status/1315700000735850496?s=20. (Image reproduced courtesy of Anab Jain's Design Investigations Project)

22 October 2020

I have been reading intermittently and in no particular order:

Maggie Nelson, *Bluets* (2017).
Susan Sontag, *Illness as Metaphor* (2013). I appreciate and admire Sontag's rigorousness, but I feel that I cannot relate because she is so rational about her pain.
Elaine Scarry, *The Body in Pain. Unmaking and Making of the World* (1985).

At the moment I can only read and fully become immersed in Nelson's writing. It feels like she is speaking to me intimately. That is strange because she does not decant her feelings to the reader. The author and reader are engaged in a relationship of civic formal intimacy as in Roland Barthes' *Camera Lucida* (2000) or *A Lover's Discourse* (2002).

Nelson writes in paragraphs. They are numbered, as if they are propositions. This Wittgensteinian style is well suited to someone as nimble and meticulous as Nelson. But, in fact, they are more vignettes than logical propositions. Reading and composing in small paragraphs makes sense for my pandemic, injury-shaped, scattered brain. My current preference would be to write a chapter in 222 characters. My desk is full with little post-it stickies.

I underlined some passages from Nelson's *Bluet* for this writing exercise. This following paragraph is lovely and grandiose and truthful (unacademic words, but accurate here, I think). She seems to know and feel her friend's unshareable pain but also folds the exteriority of her ability to share pain back into her friend's generous '*within*':

> 104. I do not feel my friend's pain, but when I unintentionally cause her pain I wince as if I hurt somewhere, and I do. Often in exhaustion I lay my head down on her lap in her wheel chair and tell her how much I love her, that I'm so sorry she is in so much pain, pain I can witness and imagine but that I do not know. She says, if anyone knows this pain besides me, it is you (and J, her lover). This is generous, for to be close to her pain has always felt like a privilege to me, even though pain could be defined as that which we typically aim to avoid. Perhaps this is because she remains so generous *within* hers, and because she has never held any hierarchy of grief, either before her accident or after, which seems to me nothing less than a form of enlightenment. (Nelson, 2017, p. 39, original emphasis)

Companions are friends who know what they don't know and who know that pain cannot be shared.

* * *

Where does bodily interiority end; where does the exterior world start? Nelson writes:

> 109. Over time my injured friend's feet have become blue and smooth from disuse ... Often we examine parts of her body together, as if their paralysis has rendered them objects of inquiry independent of us both. But they are still hers. No matter what happens to our bodies in our lifetimes, no matter if they become like 'pebbles in water,' they remain ours; us, theirs. (Nelson, 2017, p. 42)

As I read this passage, I remember a boy from summer school. He walked barefoot around town. He said that his feet were not 'part of his body'. I knew back then that it was supposed to be a cultural or political statement of some sort. Feeling no pain. The sole of the feet, as if they were shoes, were abandoned to the external world. I remember feeling sorry for his feet because I felt that he was treating his feet and by extension, the world, with little compassion.

At this point, I come to think my problem with the notion of the body within the context of legal theory is that it is so unspecific to denote anything and nothing. It can be material, immaterial, meaning an organism, or its parts. It can be an organon, an organ, a vessel, an agent. The two bodies of the king. The office and the bodily incarnation. The bodies can multiply (post-election observation, 9 November 2020). At the moment, there are three bodies with the US president elect, current president not conceding and the office of the president to be occupied.

23 October 2020

Do I take a view on these contradicting and multiple notions of a 'body'? I am not interested in functions of body and its liminalities, but more what is happening *inside* it right now, *within* the boundaries of my skin 'below' which is invisible to the outside, but which preoccupies and bounds me.

I am feeling a bit lost with the huge, vague concept that I am supposed to write hypothetically about. The contradiction between the speculative exercise and my embodied reality seems overwhelming: this strange task of as-if-writing is clashing with the persistent throbbing pain in my upper body. The more my body is preoccupied with attending to or willing away pain, the more I feel that words and other modalities of representing thought elude me. The gap between my experienced reality and finding a truthful language for it is frustrating.

The literary critic Merve Emre writes about the opposite end of the pain spectrum: 'the pain of precision'. It comes up in a very different context of her review of Ingeborg Bachmann's work, but it is strangely relevant to my question about how one can express oneself and communicate with others through language if pain is essentially unshareable.[6] Here, 'pain' seems to be a loose translation and derivation from Paul Celan's words to Bachmann as *peinlich genau*. Emre writes (2020):

> If the pain of precision comes from the desire to speak with absolute clarity, then its embarrassment surfaces from the impossibility of perfect understanding: the failure to anticipate another's reading, the vulnerability of realizing that one's mind has been breached by another's thoughts, the confusion of emotion that makes exactness both more urgent and more unattainable.

In its ordinary German meaning, the adjective *peinlich* denotes more an affect of embarrassment, however etymologically it might be related to 'pain'. Embarrassment or frustration is not the same kind of pain as the numbing, throbbing pain, or the acute electric nerve pain that flashes through the body. Yet, it is true that imprecision and a lack of language have both physical and affective implications. When we think about the function and consequences of legal language, there is so much at stake. Can legal or medical language approximate pain? It does so through metaphors. Nelson writes:

[6] One editor asks about my sources and use of literary references. I did not have a research plan or literature review for this piece for the reasons that I have explained and also because the initial brief for the contribution was to provide a personal reflection on the writing process. I find that much thinking happens when reading, listening, watching, without a particular aim. Research questions seem to gestate in the back of the mind without overtly taking the centre stage; fragments of arguments make random sideways appearances rather than linearly or step by step. In the first year of the pandemic, my access to books in the library shrank radically. I owe immense thanks to my literary friends online who have sustained me with wonderful reading materials during my period of injury.

> 182. In the Phaedrus, the written word is also notoriously called pharmakon. The question up for debate between Socrates and Phaedrus is whether the written word kills memory or aids it—whether it cripples the mind's power, or whether it cures it of its forgetfulness. Given the multiple meanings of pharmakon, the answer is, in a sense, a matter of translation. (Nelson, 2017, p. 72)

I have been so reliant on the written word, on writing generally, as *pharmakon*, but with the limited ability to use my right upper limb, I am wondering if the reliance on writing has crippled me mentally and physically. What have I lost as a result of my reliance on writing and the written word; what would it take to untrain myself from the reliance on writing as a thinking tool and as a memory aid; why do I remember sounds and spoken word less clearly; is it a zero-sum process, hearing versus seeing? But then why do I remember scents and smells (affective atmospheres) better than words?

Such a 'matter of translation', as the written word or *pharmakon*, can represent the opposite of cure because it can erase the memory of pain when it mispresents the pain or translates it wrongly. This would result in a double injury of misrepresentation: the injustice and the causing of more pain, or intensifying it, when powerful institutions (law, medicines) mispresent individual bodily pain and objectify it wrongly and durably (e.g. doctor's reports, court judgments).

26 October 2020

> The simplest characteristic of pain is its capacity to force the attention, to distract, to deny freedom. (Valéry)[7]

The pain is less domineering when I am in a horizontal position or in water. At least it seems that my brain feels supported more kindly. I cannot offer any reason for this. Truman Capote said in a 1957 Paris Review interview that he was very much a 'horizontal writer'. I do not compare myself with him in any way, but I agree that most of my writing and thinking has occurred on the couch or in bed, or in one of those very comfortable reading-room chairs in the British Library that supported my body perfectly.

I want to read a history of anaesthetics. The practice of anaesthetics is an interesting junction where pain becomes classified and represented into chemicals and quantified dosage. I bookmark Isabelle Baszanger (1998) *Inventing Pain Medicine: From the Laboratory to the Clinic.* The academic hive mind on chronic pain also recommends Lucie Dalibert (2016) 'Living with Spinal Cord Stimulation: Doing Embodiment and Incorporation'.

[7] *Cahiers*, 2000 (orig 1973), 'Affectivity'.

28 October 2020

I am thinking about my irritation (?), disappointment (?) with some theorists who had rushed to reduce the pandemic to their existing theoretical frameworks (Agamben, Latour, Žižek). Does the world really need the unlocking of the 'bigger truth' on the pandemic by theorists, when the queering that theorising would need is not yet possible because we literally don't know our positions ourselves, as it feels like the grounds on which we stand are moving and yielding? Why would one want to foreclose the possibility of interpretation so hurriedly instead of waiting to see the pandemic unfolding in very uneven and unequal ways? Perhaps it might not be best explained by reference to existing concepts of 'network', 'state of exception,' or a 'barbarism versus civilization'.

All I want to read right now is anthropology of pandemics and zoonosis and science pre-prints that come out daily like hot doughnuts from the deep fryer of PubMed database.

Catherine Malabou wrote in March 2020 about the difficulty of thinking and working during the pandemic. Whereas some have been able to compartmentalise the pandemic as an 'outside' and have become extra productive and more certain in their theoretical orientation (as she describes them: 'I admire those who are able to analyze the current crisis caused by the covid-19 pandemic in terms of global politics, capitalism, the state of exception, ecological crisis, China-Us-Russia strategic relationships, etc.'), she diagnoses her sense of disorientation as a loss of capacity to withdraw into oneself, and thus interprets it as a loss of interiority. In response, she tries to carve out a space for herself. So, paradoxically, for Malabou, the epidemic quarantine becomes only tolerable when seeking confinement from confinement:

> Personally, at the moment, I am on the contrary trying to be an 'individual.' This, once again, is not out of any individualism but because I think on the contrary that an *epoché*, a suspension, a bracketing of sociality, is sometimes the only access to alterity, a way to feel close to all the isolated people on Earth. (Malabou, 2020)

Her writing is more generous and reflective of the feeling of disorientation and the vulnerability of not even knowing the direction of futurity. Reading her turning-away from attempts of large-scale and broad-brushed theorising, I am also reminded of McKenzie Wark's comment on the failure of grand narratives and what ought to come in its place:

> Whereas the bare minimum i think u can say is that after the failure of the grand narratives, they can't really be restarted in a more overtly Hegelian language. It turns out that just erases the difference of every body in the name of the universals of the subject and the real.
>
> Rather, one has to start with the specificities of the bodies acting in and against various institutional forms: factory, prison, school, etc. And start not just from

> the sovereignty of the body that works, but also the one that fucks, that aborts, that transitions, etc.[8]

But I disagree that the body is always sovereign. Pain is.

Addendum June 2021: one editor asks here, 'do you really mean to claim that pain is always sovereign?' I think in this diaristic writing from October 2020, I meant it in its full particularity from the viewpoint of my personal experience. The editor correctly adds nuance about minor pains, blurred pains, receding pain. I don't disagree. But this piece is not a piece of comprehensive research, but an essay which asks me to externalise the process of thinking and writing. I am not sure that any of my sentences here ought to be understood as claims. On the day of writing, complex academic truth was not be truthful or meaningful to me in relation to my experience of a particular pain.

3 November 2020

My QiGong and yoga teacher, Maymay Knight, says things that makes me think differently about the body. A few weeks ago it was 'Listen to your body', which is an over-used phrase that I have heard often but haven't really thought about. How is it possible that 'to listen', a verb used for auditory sensation and perception, can be applied and made to reconcile with the body which involves the locus of many different sensations? But we also somehow know what it means.

Another one: 'As the world is full of change that we have no power over, enjoy the constancy of your body.' But my body is in change right now, as is the world (today is the day of US elections, Vienna and Kabul are in post-terrorist trauma). The memory of what my body felt like when it felt good seems deceptive. I wonder if the memory of goodness was based on the memory of feeling fit and able. But what if that state will never come back?

13 November 2020

My line of academic work, especially digitised research and teaching in pandemic times, is mostly sedentary. Thinking is presumed to be a cerebral activity, and some think of the body as a prison for the mind to 'overcome'. But it is by now generally accepted knowledge in neuroscience that the brain is embodied. Also the body 'thinks' together with the head, particularly through a gut–brain interaction (Wood et al., 1999).

It seems to me that the body is not the real culprit for the situation I find myself in. The supposedly disembodied work is the problem.

Liz MacFall, a sociologist of markets in Edinburgh, posted yesterday: 'Academia, worse for your health than corporeal labour in a poisonous

[8] chica marx @mckenziewark, 3 June 2019 https://twitter.com/mckenziewark/status/1135360067040157702?s=20 accessed 5 July 2021.

atmosphere.'[9] She included a morbidity table for different occupations in Manchester from the mid-nineteenth century and its textual interpretation in an insurance actuary journal. I am stunned that actuaries in Victorian times knew what seems to be hushed up in our academic labour, year 2020. I had heard before that 'sitting kills', but how can I not sit when all of the marking, meetings and readings are now online? The actuary article finds sedentary work to be more poisonous than working in the mines and more 'detrimental to life':

> The highest rank [of vitality] is occupied by agricultural labourers; the lowest rank is occupied by those in the occupation of clerks. The highest degree of vitality belongs to the class whose corporeal powers are the most exercised; the lowest degree of vitality belongs to the class whose corporeal powers are least exercised ... the vitality of clerks is lower than that of painters, potters, and miners; that is to say, an occupation involving no corporeal labour is apparently more detrimental to life than occupations involving corporeal labour in a poisoned atmosphere. (Edmonds, 1855, pp. 139–140)[10]

When I was writing my PhD, I still had to get up from my library desk, go to enquiries, run up and down the stairs, go searching in endless miles of stacks, roll the stacks, climb up a ladder, go through volumes of books and so on. Now my arm and fingers are trying to coordinate millimetres of cursor movement to place the comment in the right place for an exam feedback on an online platform, and we do this for twelve hours a day for five days for three weeks.

Will my work kill me, I wonder? Do I need to pursue a different occupation to lower my morbidity rate? I wonder how much the demands of our sedentary work, especially in times of almost exclusive screen-based teaching, research and communication, are 'detrimental to life'. How much of my 'vitality' am I prepared to trade for another journal article, fifty more essays, hundred more exam markings?

I guess we are disposable bodies, particularly because the corporeal injuries are invisible, chronic, a long-time coming and hidden from the world of minds. What becomes externally visualised is the supposedly immaterial labour that goes into our work 'producing' the material 'output' of publications and teaching, whereas in reality it is our bodily interiors that pay the price.

How ridiculous would be an obituary that would say, 'She died of sedentary work.'

16 November 2020

Started to write introduction.

[9] See https://twitter.com/allartmarkets/status/1326863833185529856?s=20 accessed 5 July 2021.

[10] My thanks to Liz MacFall for sharing the reference.

20 November 2020

I think my old-white-men-theory disappointments, still hanging over me from the lockdown No. 1, are slowly dissipating in lockdown No. 2 where I currently find myself.

Twitter replies and debates that some of the posts develop into and come close to the real interaction, if not being even more direct, resembling robust and playful jostles that a good seminar or intimate workshop setting can provide in moments of shared excitement about strongly felt views on theoretical delineations and divergences. Today, there is a discussion about a critique of theoretical imperatives that Christos Lynteris, an anthropologist of epidemics and zoonosis, has just published (2020). Another anthropologist, Casper Bruun Jensen, objects to the way in which the critique is presented. I read this unfolding debate as exploring the ethics of interdisciplinary work and modes of critique.

Despite my irritations about vague interdisciplinary superficiality and imperative theories, I do like to wander into other countries of academic inquiry for pleasure. It's less of a reconnaissance mission, or seeking the thrill of the new, but more a wanderlust-type curiosity. This morning, starting from a lecture announcement on the not so small matter of 'Climate, Class & Capitalism's Metabolisms: A Ridiculously Brief History' by Jason W Moore, who argues for the conceptualisation of the Capitalocene rather than Anthropocene—the proliferating '-cenes' trigger another abstraction fatigue in me—I arrive at an intriguing account on Magic and Ecology @EcologyMagic and a post with an image of a fantastic yet uncanny baroque hare with antlers and sequin gloves by the artist, Charlotte Rodgers.[11] The accompanying text is by David Abram: 'The body is a place where clouds, earthworms, guitars, clucking hens, and clear-cut hillsides all converge, forging alliances, mergers, and metamorphoses.'

The body is such a battle ground, bound, but also porous and open through metabolism. Julie Livingston writes, 'healing the body requires healing the body politic—the collection of people who together form a larger whole' (2020). I agree with her too readily when she writes: 'The body is an act of exchange and a site of vulnerability in a complex and more-than-human world.' But the exchange does not seem equal. It rather resembles a one-way street. The permeability of the body stands in stark contrast to the un-shareability of bodily pain. What is sensed from the outside, seeps through our skins and metabolises (Barua et al., 2020), but what is sensed within the body's interior is difficult to express to the outside, especially if the sensation is pain.

Perhaps the body is then better understood as a dialectic organism (or form?) between closed and open. This dialectic understanding seems to lead us back to Humberto Maturana and Francisco Varela's autopoietic conception of the openness/closedness of living organisms (1991). But power in such a

[11] See https://twitter.com/EcologyMagic/status/1319551663561211904?s=20 accessed 5 July 2021.

dialectic relation is uneven; it is rather a dynamic of dominance. Legal forms of body tend to focus and privilege the former meaning of body's boundedness (human body as person, corporate body, embodiments for materialising the immaterial) rather than its porosity, openness and vulnerability.

If there is a commonality between the body politic and the body in pain, it's that they both decentre a subject's language. Language is robbed from oneself and serves as the medium for envisaging the world as abstract structures, such as market, law, network, assemblage. These structures, in turn, are seen to evolve around abstract concepts, such as capital, rights, race, citizen, migrant. Around these intangible constructs are tangible practices of exclusion and inclusion (who gets to eat what, what are our working conditions, bodies crossing or stopped at borders, hospitalisation, practices of dying) and physical materials (flesh, virus, saliva, plexiglass, palm oil, high-fructose glucose, masks, fences around student halls of residence, plastic, oil etc).

The artist Jenny Holzer wrote 'WORDS TEND TO BE INADEQUATE' as part of her *Truisms*. It feels even more true in 2020. It has also lost its irony. The sentence feels suffocating.

21 November 2020

It is 8:30 pm on a Friday, and I have just returned from the hospital. I heard some faraway techno music in the white tunnel of the MRI. In the midst of lockdown No. 2, or precisely because of it, I felt perversely happy to be in the publicness of the hospital. In the waiting lobby I looked with new eyes at other bodies, their various clothing, and leather shoes and heels. The MRI tube rail was warm with magnetic waves.

Back home, I read 'A Heaven of the Book', an essay by Ryan Ruby about the poet Friederike Mayröcker's body of work, and it moves me very much, especially this sentence: 'It is only by "writing with the body" that "life can be metamorphosed into language," and it is only by being metamorphosed into language that life survives the inevitable breakdown of the body' (Ruby, 2020).

Before the body breaks, or before the breaking point of numbing pain and death, we necessarily write *with* our body.

* * *

I think I have reached a point where I can stop collating and start the linearisation of thoughts by writing. The gestation of ideas and argument for this assignment has been more personal and chaotic than it usually is.

What would be actually useful at this point, instead of another iteration of body multiple or emergent body, is a history of an idea or epistemic history of the term 'body', a genealogy of some sort. This is better done in a PhD thesis or book project. A book chapter is not the right format for it. What I could do in the limited space of a chapter is develop an initial diagnosis of the dialectical aspects of the ways in which we use the word 'body'.

I feel ready to do the work of narrowing down the thoughts about the 'body' in law as a kind of unequal dialectics into a drawing now. Drawing allows flexibility in writing. I prefer it to a text outline because I have found out that the writing process often leads to changes in the argument, which can be more easily adapted in a drawing. Also, I like the non-linearity of drawings, which make logical relations, distances and gaps much more explicit by spatial ordering and graphics. But then the writing process might change everything again.

23 November 2020

The procedures in the hospital were rather unpleasant and the second injection was so painful that I had to reactivate birthing breathing technique again after exactly thirteen years. So much of modern medicine's pain management seems to depend on the probability calculation (aka evidence-based medicine) or belief that frontloaded pain for healing is better than unhealed chronic pain. But what do they know about how my body interior feels?

Thirteen years ago, my waters broke. Tonight, sterile water, together with some other chemical liquids, is injected into my shoulder capsule in order to dilate and rupture it. Water out, water in. A metabolism of some sort.

24 November 2020

My body gave birth to another body today thirteen years ago. I still find it wondrous that all humans co-inhabited another human body for around nine months. As far as I know, there have been no exceptions to this beginning within one shared bodily home.

References

Barthes, R. (2000 [1980]). *Camera Lucida*. Vintage.

Barthes, R. (2002 [1977]). *A Lover's Discourse: Fragments*. Vintage.

Barua, M., White, T., & Nally, D. (2020, October 1). Rescaling the Metabolic. *Crassh News*. Retrieved July 5, 2021, from http://www.crassh.cam.ac.uk/blog/post/rescaling-the-metabolic

Baszanger, I. (1998). *Inventing Pain Medicine: From the Laboratory to the Clinic*. Rutgers University Press.

Chee, A. (2018). *How to Write an Autobiographical Novel: Essays*. Mariner Books.

Clark, A. (1998). *Being There: Putting Brain, Body, and World Together Again*. Bradford/MIT Books.

Dalibert, L. (2016). Living with Spinal Cord Stimulation: Doing Embodiment and Incorporation. *Science, Technology and Human Values, 41*(4), 635–659.

Damasio, A. (2003). *Looking for Spinoza: Joy, Sorrow and the Feeling Brain*. Harcourt.

Edmonds, T. (1855). On the Laws of Morality and Sickness of the Labouring Classes of England. *The Assurance Magazine and Journal of the Institute of Actuaries, 5*, 127–145.

Emre, M. (2020, October 22). The Meticulous One. *New York Review of Books*. Retrieved July 5, 2020, from https://www.nybooks.com/articles/2020/10/22/ingeborg-bachmann-meticulous-one/

Grosz, E. (1994). *Volatile Bodies*. Indiana University Press.

Haraway, D. (2007). *When Species Meet*. University of Minnesota Press.

Hayles, N. K. (2005). *My Mother Was a Computer*. University of Chicago Press.

Hoffmann, C. (2013). Processes on Paper: Writing Procedures as Non-material Research Devices. *Science in Context, 26*, 279–303.

Kang, H. Y. (2012). Science Inside Law. *Science in Context, 25*(4), 551–594.

Kang, H. Y. (2018). Law's Materiality: Between Concrete Matters and Abstract Forms, or How Matter Becomes Material. In Philippopoulos-Mihalopoulous, A. (Ed.), *Routledge Handbook for Law and Theory*. Routledge.

Kang, H. Y., & Kendall, S. (2019). Introduction. Special issue on 'Legal Materiality' *Law Text Culture*, 23, 1–15.

Kant, I. (1998). *Critique of Pure Reason*. Cambridge University Press.

Khoury, E. (2017). The Art of Fiction. No. 233. *Paris Review, 220*(Spring) https://www.theparisreview.org/interviews/6940/the-art-of-fiction-no-233-elias-khoury

Livingston, J. (2020, November 19). To Heal the Body, Heal the Body Politic. *Public Books*. Retrieved July 5, 2021, from https://www.publicbooks.org/to-heal-the-body-heal-the-body-politic

Lynteris, C. (2020). The Imperative Origins of Covid-19. *L'Homme, 234*(235), 21–31. Retrieved July 5, 2021, from https://www.cairn.info/revue-l-homme-2020-2-page-21.htm

Malabou, C. (2020, March 23). To Quarantine from Quarantine: Rousseau, Robinson Crusoe, and "I". *In the Moment*. Retrieved July 5, 2021, from https://critinq.wordpress.com/2020/03/23/to-quarantine-from-quarantine-rousseau-robinson-crusoe-and-i/

Maturana, H., & Varela, F. (1991). *Autopoiesis and Cognition*. D Reidel/Springer.

Nelson, M. (2015). *Argonauts*. Graywolf Press.

Nelson, M. (2017 [2009]). *Bluets*. Jonathan Cape.

Rotman, B. (2008). *Becoming beside Ourselves: The Alphabet, Ghosts, and Distribute Human Beings*. Duke University Press.

Ruby, R. (2020, November 23). A Heaven of the Book. *Poetry Foundation*. Retrieved July 5, 2021, from https://www.poetryfoundation.org/articles/154848/a-heaven-of-the-book

Scarry, E. (1985). *The Body in Pain: The Making and Unmaking of the World*. Oxford University Press.

Sontag, S. (2013 [1977]). Illness as Metaphor. In D. Rieff (Ed.), *Susan Sontag: Essays of the 1960s and 1970s* (pp. 675–729). Library of America.

Stafford, B. (2001). *Visual Analogy*. MIT Press.

Tsing, A. (2015). *The Mushroom at the End of the World: On the Possibilities of Life in Capitalist Ruins*. Princeton University Press.

Valéry, P. (2000). *Cahiers*. Peter Lang, 1.

Wood, J. D., Alpers, D. H., & Andrews, P. L. R. (1999). Fundamentals of Neurogastroenterology. *Gut, 45*, II6–II16.

CHAPTER 9

Afterword

Davina Cooper

Abstract This afterword reflects on the interdisciplinary methodologies and concept of the body to emerge in this book to explore three themes. First, it considers the embodied academic, particularly in relation to aging and remembering. Second, it addresses the conceptual reach of the body and considers the use of embodiment to describe non-human formations, such as the state. Third, it considers the political implications of extending the concept of the body to very different kinds of formation. It suggests that the stakes in how the body is conceptualised depend on purpose, which can also be a methodological purpose. Conceptual equivalence may be more useful when thinking is oriented towards an imagined hopeful future than when, critically, understanding the power relations and inequalities that currently operate.

Keywords State • Prefigurative • Academic memory

A book about a book about the body. I want to reflect on some of the methodological, ethical, and conceptual issues raised when the body becomes the prompt to consider how research, analysis, and writing are done—when the interiority of the academic endeavour is opened and spread out. I also want to explore the body that acts as the prompt—what kind of bodies does this involve? But let me start with the challenge of writing an 'afterword' since this is a book which is, above all, about reflexive legal research. Accepting an invitation to write an afterword is a step into—if not quite the unknown—then zones of partial knowing. With some rough sense of what a book is about, it is

D. Cooper (✉)
Dickson Poon School of Law, King's College London, London, UK
e-mail: davina.cooper@kcl.ac.uk

D. Herman, C. Parsley (eds.), *Interdisciplinarities*, Palgrave Socio-Legal Studies, https://doi.org/10.1007/978-3-030-89297-5_9

a commitment to say something—to reflect on the chapters and what they might say once they have been written. It is a labour driven by curiosity and interest—what will the chapters do; what will they prompt me to think about; what embryonic ideas will be tugged; what new terrain may I land in? Specifically, will writing an afterword stitch together ideas I have been thinking about with ideas, and ways of framing them, that I have not yet considered?

This book is about the 'how' of doing research, pursuing the 'how' in ways that unsettle methodological orthodoxies. Too often, particularly for people beginning to undertake research, methodology appears like a set of predefined rules or pathways, where choice is limited to deciding which rules to follow or which instruction manual to take up. This book does not critique this approach directly. Instead, it sketches an alternative understanding—conveyed through being done, as contributors identify their own research paths. These paths are not so much diligently followed as formed and crafted, including with others. Interdisciplinarity here is not a goal to strive towards or an exploration of what comes from adding one subject to another. Instead, interdisciplinarity becomes the ground from which contributors write—the terrain chapters traverse—sometimes tacitly, sometimes more explicitly (e.g. see Connal Parsley's chapter), as contributors reflect on what they do in more-than-disciplinary terms. 'Recipe?' is a word I wrote, occasionally, in my notes as I read the chapters. But while the book can be read as demonstrating some new ways of mixing ingredients and processes, the chapters also trouble this reading. The intent, I think, is not to offer steps for others to stick to but, rather, to identify some ways of doing academic research. These are offered as approaches to consider and experiment with—examples of how some academics work as they develop and shape their own intellectual habits. I read this book as one that encourages readers to take confidence in their own paths, recipes, and habits, recognising that these may be (should be?) messy, disjointed, evolving, and creative.

The book is also an argument for the value in being reflexive. This does not have to be explicitly written into the text as this book does. Nevertheless, the book models the importance of reflexivity in academic thinking in two key senses. The first is an attentiveness to the *embodied* character of research. The researcher's body, in this book, is a situated body, working in archives, sitting on tribunals, undertaking field research. It is a body that can be stressed, excited, and in motion. Thanos Zartaloudis evocatively captures the affective and embodied character of research and writing—tracing the movement from despair to coffee, to skimming texts, sleeping, return to the world of living and hope, the manic collection of ideas and other thinking-prompts, and then writing. As the book describes, this is a process of slipping in and out of control; where a wildness—of not being quite reined in or exceeding what is reined in—takes up residence within the text. It is also, for many academics, a very folded experience of embodiment, taking shape inches from a computer screen. The seated body returns several times through this collection—most starkly, in Hyo Yoon Kang's comments on the reduced lifespan of the excessively sitting body. Second, reflexivity moves through this book in the choices and responsibilities that a researcher faces. Contributors foreground the ethical—as it surfaces in relation to research dilemmas: how to write about illegal practices, for instance; how to approach the subjugated body. I return to this.

While chapters demonstrate different starting points, approaches, questions, and perspectives, there is also much common ground. One site of convergence is the contributors' shared interest in working from the margins—from sites of legal subordination and liminality—including enslavement, institutional racism, cramped residential spaces, and traditional healing methods. At the level of process, chapters share a concern with unanticipated material, data, and ideas; of hearing the silences; and of iteration. Rather than working linearly from data to theory (or vice versa) and then to analysis, the chapters stress the ongoing dialogic movement between the site/example/case and the wider intellectual conversations and concerns that a selected instance speaks to (or is used to speak to), so that both parts are enriched. The site here does not function as a passive terrain spread open for theoretical or conceptual analysis (see also Cooper, 2014). Parsley describes the value of thinking through a single instance that can tell a broader story—of thinking *with* an example rather than about it. Finally, the authors share an ambition that research and analysis should take them somewhere new and unexpected, not just confirm already held thoughts or observations. Their methods are ways of pushing themselves and their analysis to go deeper, further.

This book is about the embodied doing of research, analysis, and writing. It is also about the body as a subject of analysis. Here too, the book is full of lively insights about the body as imagined, regulated, experienced, and theorised. For the most part, these are authors whose work has not explicitly and directly attended to embodiment. Thus, their turn to the body demonstrates the insights that come from approaching the body through its commodification, racialisation, dwelling, pain, healing, and supplication. I am struck, for instance, by the body shaped and squeezed in (and into) Helen Carr's discussion of the law on minimum room sizes for houses in multiple occupation—regulating what counts as too small a space for a landlord to rent out. Carr's chapter details how assumed bodily ways of living and socialising shape what counts as acceptable—the sofa bed only pulled out when a lover comes to stay. I am left with an image of distributed living, as features of domestic life in small residential spaces get contracted out to the commercial storage facility or repatriated (reparented) to the family basement or attic.

I am also struck by the chapters shared orientation towards a certain kind of body—this is a body that is human, subordinated, and vulnerable. Kang's chapter eloquently explores the body in pain. Her chapter refuses to treat this body as an object of analysis. Rather, the body-in-pain is the starting point for a powerful essay about what can be said, from this place, in conditions where pain both escapes and thwarts language's use. As a critical and progressive engagement with embodiment, contributors share a concern that the body should not become a spectacle of suffering and subjugation. Emily Haslam explores this ethical concern in relation to slavery—quoting Sadiya Hartman on 'the hyperembodiness of the powerless' (Hartman, 1997, p. 19). Parsley also addresses this point in his reflection on how slavery can be represented without relying on human bodies. He draws here on Cameron Rowland's exhibition *3 & 4 Will. IV c. 73*, which explored how the property established by slavery was preserved in British abolition law.[1]

Avoiding the fetishization of suffering while continuing to address relations of domination is not just a question of how subjugated bodies are depicted (or not depicted). It is also about agency and action—about whose bodies are represented as shaping and driving events. In different ways, Haslam, Emilie Cloatre, and Suhraiya Jivraj address the need for counter-narratives, where enslaved, racialised, and legally precarious actors are recognised as embodied subjects who collectively (and sometimes individually) struggle, resist, and oppose the *status quo*, and who contribute to the creation of new unfolding presents. Jivraj explores this in relation to university students' anti-racist practices. Drawing on Walter Mignolo and Catherine Walsh (2018), she describes their activities as 're-existence'—not just 'resistance'. Cloatre describes how traditional healers in Senegal learned from each other about how to avoid ensnarement in the regulatory net of medical practice, which would reframe their work as illegal. Cloatre explores how everyday health practices contribute to the shape that legal regulations take—by affecting how law is imagined, translated, circumvented, and otherwise operationalised. Her analysis demonstrates how state power is not fixed, but changes through the practices it encounters. In different ways, then, the book foregrounds the ethical and political choices that academics make—the care and responsibility they have—where identifying and exposing relations of power is important, but where the power available and exercised to counter domination is also important to explore.

In thinking about this collection as a book about a book about bodies, I want to make three further points. Following the book's brief, these points indicate directions I would take, today, if I was writing an afterword to a book on the concept of the body. I begin with a reflection on the embodied academic; turn to consider how the discussion of embodiment relates to non-human, non-animal bodies, and particularly to the embodied state (the focus of much of my work); and, finally, consider the divergence between a critical and prefigurative approach when it comes to the question of embodied equivalence. This last discussion asks, what is at stake, politically, in talking about both humans and states as bodies? Is this conceptual equivalence more acceptable for thinking that is oriented towards an imagined hopeful future than for critically understanding the power relations and inequalities that currently operate?

The book's focus on the embodied researcher led me to think about my own embodiment, and that took me to a set of reflections about the academic-becoming-older. Focus on aging can segue into concern about aching, physically impeded, unwell, or menopausal bodies. But, as this book explores, physical and mental bodily processes interact, fold into each other, and are

[1] See https://www.ica.art/exhibitions/cameron-rowland accessed 16 August 2021.

often indistinct. Thus, I want to use the terms of embodiment to think about the remembering academic. Memory and the challenges of the past circulate through this book in several ways. Jivraj draws on memories of racist housing practices encountered as a younger academic as she reflects on the importance of counter-storytelling in responding to experiences of racism. Other chapters address the politics of what gets remembered; and the research choices invoked in how experiences and histories get recalled and used.

My thinking on the remembering academic has been prompted by my current research into contemporary feminist politics as part of an Economic and Social Research Council-funded project on 'The Future of Legal Gender'. The project addresses the implications of abolishing sex and gender as aspects of legal personhood in Britain, primarily (although not exclusively) by removing sex from birth certificates.[2] Undertaking this research has tipped the project into a fraught political debate about the status of biological sex, and the need to engage with a contemporary branch of British feminism that demands state law treat sex as binary, immutable, and as a central driver of women's oppression.[3] Adopted by a constellation of forces, advocates argue that women are human females, who should be protected from predatory men (which seems to largely equate, in practice, to 'male strangers').

A sex-based approach to gender and feminist politics concerns me and, in large part, this concern is shaped by the feminist politics and histories I have lived through. But what place should our remembered pasts have in our academic work? Should we act as if we have not been present; should the memories we carry remain tacit ones—informing what we think but never or rarely spoken? Listening to current claims about the importance of embodied sex, I think about socialist feminists' long-standing emphasis on labour and care-work—that gender is produced through divisions of labour not from binary bodily capacities. I think about the 1980s radical feminist emphasis on heterosexuality—that people become women (and men) through their participation in heterosexualised social relations. I remember earlier ambivalence among some lesbian feminists about self-defining as women even as they criticised others who claimed they were too butch to count as women. I remember discourses of predation, in 1980s Britain, that were explicitly anti-lesbian—claiming lesbians would get their hands into women and girls' underwear. I remember the arguments made, in the early 1990s, against feminists relying on discourses of protection on the grounds such discourses reproduced racialised anxieties about vulnerable white women. And I remember the extensive debates in the

[2] The other investigators on this project are Emily Grabham, Elizabeth Peel and Flora Renz. Robyn Emerton, Han Newman and Jessica Smith were also research associates on the project.

[3] Chris Beasley and Carol Bacchi (2007, 2012) offer a better way of being attuned to embodiment in their turn to 'social flesh'. This term provides, for them, a way of thinking about the 'social' that pays attention to bodies, while stressing the importance of the social to how embodiment is imagined—'a more substantive way of gripping together the corporeal and the socio-political—of grasping simultaneously the sociality of flesh and the physicality of social life' (Beasley & Bacchi, 2012, p. 105).

1990s about essentialism and whether women, as a group, shared anything in common. But, in wondering what to do with these memories, I also remember long-running concerns about how age can be used to silence others: 'we know *how it is* because we know *how it was*'; even as feminism has paid episodic attention to the biases that discount older women's knowledge and presence (e.g. MacDonald & Rich, 1984).

Running through this book are different sources of knowledge—archival, experiential, empirical, professional—and the book attends to the claims and authority that these sources confer. Older bodies are interesting as sites of vulnerability (of challenged, adjusting, dismissed bodies), while simultaneously being associated with cultural capital, where remembering is often associated with illegitimate deployment of the latter. There is an extensive and interesting literature on memory and forgetting, including in work on critical nostalgia (e.g. Tannock, 1995; Cashman, 2006; Pickering & Keightley, 2006). The remembering academic body, of course, is not a source of pure, clean knowing—but then, nor are other sources. Memory gets deployed and pulled in specific directions and managed for specific uses. But so, too, do other sources of knowing. While it is often seen as wrongly silencing and de-authorising the newcomer body, long-timers and recent entrants together provide interesting sources of insight and knowledge. Focusing reflexively on the embodied researcher, in all its different guises, is important. The risk, otherwise, is that the embodied researcher becomes an already determined set of issues to address: the dilemma of academic status and authority; one's location across different axes of inequality (as if inequality was an axis). Oriented away from rules and orthodoxies, this book points to the importance of approaching reflexivity in other ways—to work from actual embodied feelings, including of uncertainty. While such feelings are informed by existing debates and accounts of reflexivity, they benefit from not being reined in or limited by them.

The second theme I would explore, in an afterword to an interdisciplinary book on the concept of the body, concerns non-human bodies and the challenge of equivalence, when bodily terms are used for both human and non-human entities. One thing that struck me, on reading this collection, was how discussion angles away from desiring, pleasured, happy bodies, from (non-human) animal bodies, and from other kinds of institutional bodies. These latter are briefly mentioned. Jivraj's discussion of racialised bodies, for instance, brings other bodies into the frame, including the university, its faculties, and bodies of knowledge. But what is politically at stake in talking about both biological and non-biological bodies (if we can use this language to instantiate the distinction) in similar terms?

The language of embodiment has long been used to explore political and governmental formations. Claire Rasmussen and Michael Brown (2005, pp. 473–474) describe how early accounts of the body politic presented the state as a composite, hierarchically ordered formation, with the prince or king as its head, the military as its arms and hands, and peasants as its feet (see also Neocleous, 2003). Subsequent representations have explored how the bodies of presidents, dead soldiers, 'terrorists' and others represent and stand in for the state or the ambition for a state (see Laderman, 1997; Dumm, 1998; Hawley, 2005).[4] This image of enfoldment and substitution sits alongside another historic narrative, one Kang and Parsley refer to. This is the 'king's two bodies' (Kantorowicz, 2016 [1957]) where the temporary, mortal body of the sovereign is sutured to the perpetual political body it temporarily has charge of. The relationship between the two has a contemporary salience too. I am reminded of this rewatching (through Covid-19 lockdown) the long-running American television series on the US presidency, *The West Wing*, alongside the more recent show on the British royal establishment, *The Crown*.

Is the language of embodiment helpful when used across such different phenomena? This can get posed as a conceptual dilemma—whether to craft concepts in broad or narrow ways given the analytical implications of linking things together or emphasising their differences. Kang, for instance, asks whether the notion of the body risks becoming so general and unspecific that it can mean everything and nothing. This is also a political question. How are states and law seen and approached when they are framed, for instance, as affective and vulnerable bodies—where embodiment identifies the continuous process of shape-taking with its material, sensory, and imaginary aspects that are simultaneously both organised and disorganised? Embodiment can capture relations of precarity and dissolution. It can also entrench a conception of formations as (or as oriented to being) unified, hierarchical, and agentic. In this vein, Mark Neocleous (2003, p. 38) criticises the conceptual application of body-talk to the state: 'The corporeal metaphor is an ideological tool aimed at achieving good order and locating sovereignty … it is for this reason that the corporeal model is a dead end for any critical politics of radical transformation.'

Embodiment can also suggest boundedness and separation from an outside that is adjacent and touching. While this understanding has been extensively criticised by feminists and others, depicting bodies instead as porous, permeable, fluctuating, and heterogeneous, with changing or ill-defined borders (e.g. see Grosz, 1994; Shildrick, 2000), Kang's discussion of the body-in-pain provides an interesting counterpoint. Kang urges us to understand how pain individualises and closes off the experience of the body. Pain may be shaped and sourced by external processes, but the interior sensation is a solitary and lonely one. Kang's account does not suggest that the body is *really* closed rather than open. However, her account, anchored in the body-in-pain, directs us away from the body—whether state or animal—as a thing before us that can be properly and fully known. Returning to the body as a concept, how we think about the body depends on our purpose and methodology—what we are taking up the language of the body for.

When it comes to the state and law, the language of embodiment has different consequences when used for critical as opposed to prefigurative scholarship. For critical research, the language of embodiment, *when it becomes a language*

[4] I have explored more progressive versions of state embodiment in Cooper (2013).

of equivalence between very different kinds of entities, seems problematic. This is not because some entities are properly bodies and others are not; or because entities are held apart in stable fixed ways. Zartaloudis and Haslam describe how law re-encodes (metamorphosises) human bodies; how it captures and remakes them in and into legal processes including in the form of remedies (Haslam discusses *habeas corpus*). But this plasticity does not mean there is an equivalence of power, force, experience, or feeling between human and state bodies (as we currently know them to be). This point comes through vividly in Haslam's discussion of the commodification of enslaved peoples. Her analysis relies on the important distinction between human and other kinds of bodies—especially those we conventionally think of as inanimate. Humans should not be treated as property, while some other kinds of things, perhaps, can be. Jivraj's critical account of universities not listening to students' stories of racism makes a related point. Universities not listening to students does not seem analogous to students not listening to universities telling stories of their (financial) pain. The suffering state is not the same as a suffering human. A state that sticks to human subjects or dwells within them is not analogous to a democratic conception of humans composing states. Humans playing is not the same as the state playing and so on (see Cooper, 2019). Critique of the corporation as a legal person operates along similar lines. Treating human and commercial entities as if they are equivalents misrecognises both the distinct power of corporations and the distinct sensory life and political entitlements of humans.

My point here is not that critical work should necessarily avoid the rich conceptual language of embodiment when discussing commercial and state formations. But since the language of embodiment can create equivalences, the work done by this equivalence-making matters. This work is not singular and uniform. In academic contexts, methodology and orientation come into play. This becomes apparent in considering a second methodological perspective, prompted by this book. This perspective, which I will call a prefigurative conceptual perspective, urges us to think about what bodies, and different kinds of bodies, *could come to mean and be* (see also Beasley & Bacchi, 2012, p. 107). Prefigurative conceptualising, as a method which embodies, in the present, desired meanings associated with possible futures, is not discussed directly. Nevertheless, the prefigurative orientation of the 'as if' runs through the book. Parsley describes how he deliberately takes up a preferred interpretation *as if* it were self-evident rather than presenting it as a contingent reading anchored in a particular framework. More generally, the book tasks contributors with a fiction—of acting *as if* they were writing a chapter on the body. In the process, they reflect on the analysis of the body that they are simultaneously both writing and not writing. Carr describes it as writing a prelude to a piece of work while reflecting on an imagined research process.

Prefigurative approaches have limitations when they work to mask the differentials of power and pain that exist. But prefiguration is part of a progressive repertoire of research methods. Here, thinking about the body of the state or of law, prefiguratively, means *turning towards the possibility* of an equivalence with other kinds of bodies (see Cooper, 2019). We might draw on the metamorphosis that Zartaloudis discusses, to consider ways of imagining state and law where neither institutional formation exerts a dominating authority and control; where both can, more easily, be viewed in sensory and acrobatic entanglements with other kinds of bodies (including human/animal ones). Considering state and law as embodied in non-hierarchical ways—as enfolding, touching, listening, and co-constituting bodies drives us to think about the forms such a state and law might take. And, here, I want to draw on Zartaloudis's chapter where he mentions supplication. Zartaloudis considers supplication through its use in Ancient Greek thought. Here, I take up its modern everyday meaning to ask, should state and law become supplicants in their relations with living humans? What on earth would this entail?

The subordination of humans, placed *below* state and law, is a familiar and troubling trope. Supplication can also be found in relations between states with vast differences of power, as well as in contemporary state relations with powerful transnational corporations. This brings intuitive appeal to the image of state and law in supplication before subordinated and marginalised bodies (although would they then be subordinated and marginal?). But what this also raises are the *embodied* geometries of state and law in this supplication. What could it mean to imagine and enact state and law *below* rather than above other embodied subjects? Not in a beneath-the-ground image of some secular hell but in ways that recall the figure of a living 'safety net'. The safety net was a longstanding idiom for the welfare state—tacitly invoked in Carr's discussion of law's responsibility in determining minimum floor space for shared rental housing. Today, in Britain, we do not hear much about the safety-net state, spread octopus-like beneath a country's inhabitants and those others who are affected by its actions. Bodies are supposed to act and to thrive, more effectively, without a safety net—at least human bodies are. Neoliberal states seem to prefer to spread their nets below corporations.

Yet, whether they are human, corporate, or state, bodies do not just exist—including in relation to each other. Bodies are worked at; and bodies undertake work. Deliberately reforming, in progressive ways, how law and state are embodied, including in their relation to other bodies, is (to say the least) a challenging task. What this book very nicely explores are some of the political challenges such body-work entails, and the different contributions that law makes to this process.

References

Beasley, C., & Bacchi, C. (2007). Envisaging a New Politics for an Ethical Future: Beyond Trust, Care and Generosity—Towards an Ethic of Social Flesh. *Feminist Theory, 8*(3), 279–298.

Beasley, C., & Bacchi, C. (2012). Making Politics Fleshly: The Ethic of Social Flesh. In A. Bletsas & C. Beasley (Eds.), *Engaging with Carol Bacchi: Strategic Interventions and Exchanges*. University of Adelaide Press.

Cashman, R. (2006). Critical Nostalgia and Material Culture in Northern Ireland. *Journal of American Folklore, 119*(472), 137–160.
Cooper, D. (2013). Public Bodies: Conceptualising Active Citizenship and the Embodied State. In S. Roseneil (Ed.), *Beyond Citizenship?: Feminism and the Transformation of Belonging*. Palgrave Macmillan.
Cooper, D. (2014). *Everyday Utopias: The Conceptual Life of Promising Spaces*. Duke University Press.
Cooper, D. (2019). *Feeling like a State: Desire, Denial, and the Recasting of Authority*. Duke University Press.
Dumm, T. L. (1998). Leaky Sovereignty: Clinton's Impeachment and the Crisis of Infantile Republicanism. *Theory and Event, 2*(4). Online.
Grosz, E. (1994). *Volatile Bodies: Toward a Corporeal Feminism*. Indiana University Press.
Hartman, S. (1997). *Scenes of Subjection: Terror, Slavery and Self-making in Nineteenth-Century America*. Oxford University Press.
Hawley, T. M. (2005). *The Remains of War*. Duke University Press.
Kantorowicz, E. (2016 [1957]). *The King's Two Bodies*. Princeton University Press.
Laderman, G. (1997). The Body Politic and the Politics of Two Bodies: Abraham and Mary Todd Lincoln in Death. *Prospects, 22*, 109–132.
MacDonald, B., & Rich, C. (1984). *Look Me in the Eye: Old Women, Aging and Ageism*. Women's Press.
Mignolo, W. D., & Walsh, C. E. (2018). On Decoloniality. Concepts, Analytics, Praxis. In W. D. Mignolo & C. E. Walsh (Eds.), *On Decoloniality* (pp. 1–12). Duke University Press.
Neocleous, M. (2003). *Imagining the State*. Open University Press.
Pickering, M., & Keightley, E. (2006). The Modalities of Nostalgia. *Current Sociology, 54*(6), 919–941.
Rasmussen, C., & Brown, M. (2005). The Body Politic as Spatial Metaphor. *Citizenship Studies, 9*(5), 469–484.
Shildrick, M. (2000). Becoming Vulnerable: Contagious Encounters and the Ethics of Risk. *The Journal of Medical Humanities, 21*(4), 215–227.
Tannock, S. (1995). Nostalgia Critique. *Cultural Studies, 9*(3), 453–464.

GPSR Compliance
The European Union's (EU) General Product Safety Regulation (GPSR) is a set of rules that requires consumer products to be safe and our obligations to ensure this.

If you have any concerns about our products, you can contact us on

ProductSafety@springernature.com

In case Publisher is established outside the EU, the EU authorized representative is:

Springer Nature Customer Service Center GmbH
Europaplatz 3
69115 Heidelberg, Germany

www.ingramcontent.com/pod-product-compliance
Ingram Content Group UK Ltd.
Pitfield, Milton Keynes, MK11 3LW, UK
UKHW022001270726
14060UKWH00003B/627

* 9 7 8 3 0 3 0 8 9 2 9 6 8 *